Love

Beyond Blame

Geoff Reed

Yellow Rose Publishing Ltd

First published in United Kingdom in 2015 by

Yellow Rose Publishing Ltd

A CIP catalogue record for this title is available from the British Library

ISBN 978-0-9574098-2-8

Printed and bound by Lightning Source UK Ltd

DISCLAIMER

I have tried to recreate events, locales and conversations from my memories of them. In order to maintain their anonymity in some instances I have changed the names of individuals and may have changed some identifying characteristics.

Dedicated to:

Lewis and Gavin;

Everything I am; always.

ACKNOWLEDGEMENTS

Re-visiting the huge stack of Diaries which detailed every single occurrence over a predominantly dark decade was a daunting task. A task that became a huge cathartic release for me as well as hopefully putting the answers the boys would want in the future into a better form than just diaries filled with dates, times and feelings. Along the way I received a huge amount of help and support from a great number of people, you know who you are and thank you.

There are however a few people whom I would like to specifically thank:

All the staff at National Police Training, thank you all so much for the help and guidance through tough times.

Peter, I can't and probably never will be able to thank you enough. You made a real difference to Gavin, and had a hugely positive impact on me too, thank you.

Thank you to Anya Stevenson for the original water colour for the front cover. You were attentive and delivered a beautiful illustration, exactly right and fitting to my story.

Melony thank you so much for having faith in my story and for your constant support on the journey to publication.

With Special Thanks that need to be said separately to,

Lewis and Gavin, I can't begin to explain my nervousness as I handed each one of you a manuscript for the first time. I knew that some of these words would take you back to unpleasant places, and I dearly hoped you would find answers and some understanding to enable you to truly move on. I knew that you alone would be my judges, so I thank you for the grace and courage you showed in giving me the go ahead to publish this, my story of our journey.

My Dad, Jack. Sadly gone now but I know he would have been proud of whom Lewis and Gavin have become. I hope too that he would have agreed with the stance I took. Without his influence as I grew, I doubt I would have had the strength to keep my dignity throughout. I miss you.

My dearest friend Paul, I will be forever in your debt. You showed me so much and you taught me even more, yet you never judged me. Your genuine warmth and kindness is an example to us all. We all have much to thank you for, and I know that I am a better person for having had you in my life. RIP my friend.

Join Geoff Reed on Facebook:
Love Beyond Blame – Keeping Kids Central
www.facebook.com/2015LBB

PROLOGUE

This story is about a journey, my journey and that of those around me. About terrible deep sadness and tearful profound joy. About utter helplessness followed by invincibility. Only to return to each time and again, like a hamster on a wheel. Who knows why, but like the hamster I just kept going.

This is my story of love in its differing forms, of fight and dogged determination not to be beaten, but above all it's about honesty. Honest in the reasons for the desire to win custody, honest with myself that I was truly capable and honest about my emotions. I do not seek to apportion blame or to take credit.

In writing this I have chosen to wear my wounds on the outside so everyone can see me for what and who I am, and hopefully understand me as nothing more than a father.

My feelings, emotions and above all strength, are all about this father's love and drive.

This isn't exclusively for fathers or about fathers but in my case though it clearly is, because I am one. I couldn't and wouldn't try to take a mother's stand point. This is about the depth of love that all parents feel deep within themselves.

These feelings and emotions could be felt by anyone, here is my journey…

DECISIONS

Wincing with pain as the doctor removed the infection from my foot. He finished and calmly sat on the edge of the treatment table and said "The challenge is over for you; your foot has been traumatised. The hills and the event will still be here next year, but your foot may not if you try anything stupid like carrying on."

He smiled and left the room, leaving the nurse to dress my foot, after which she handed me a prescription and a pair of crutches. The doctor's words made an impact in the short term but what I didn't know, as this challenge ended, that the greatest challenge of my life was soon to start. This would be a challenge that was to test every fibre of my heart, soul and indeed my mind.

The infection had taken root some three days earlier; peat bog water had splashed over my walking boots and into my open blisters. I'd tried several times to re-dress them, but the constant walking kept removing which ever style of dressing I tried.

My friends and travelling companions Dave and John were backpacking on the "Great Outdoors Challenge" with me. We were walking from the West coast to the East coast, across the Scottish Highlands, in just two weeks. We were a week into the event when we arrived in Newtonmore earlier that day, intending to spend one night at a hostel. But I was in a great deal of pain with my foot, which had swollen and discoloured, so a visit to the doctor's in Kingussie was my only option.

Whilst I had been having fun in the surgery, Dave and John had gone into the village to stock up on supplies for the next three-day phase through the Cairngorm Mountains to Braemar. I hobbled into the village on crutches and eventually met up with them in one of the village pubs, their faces said it all. Our threesome was now a duo and a deeply subdued atmosphere enveloped the hostel that evening as the full realisation hit us all that Dave and John would be continuing without me.

The event was over for me, for this year at least. I have to admit to a tear or two the following morning as I woke late from a drug induced sleep to find that Dave and John had gone. They had a long day in front of them so an early start was needed but I on the other hand, was to spend another week in the hostel, doped out of my head on painkillers and antibiotics and having daily visits from the district nurse to check and re-dress my foot. Indeed it was to be a week before I could walk on my foot again and I wish to register at this stage my eternal thanks to Kathryn and Peter Main, owners of Newtonmore Hostel for the kindness, caring and generosity shown to me during my enforced stay. Two finer people one could not hope to meet in such a crisis.

I flew home a week later and headlong into the decade from hell. A decade during which I was to visit many dark, tortuous places, fight battles on so many fronts and be pursued for everything including it seemed, the very air I breathed. A decade during which I would examine, in microscopic detail, my own fears, hopes and values and lay them open, on numerous occasions for personal, private and indeed public examination. I discovered reserves of strength I never dreamed I had as well as a deep understanding of myself and what makes me tick.

I discovered how to talk, how to show emotion and learned that it is never wrong to admit to hurting, no matter how deep, and that there is great strength to be gained by showing these feelings to those who genuinely care for you. I was continually hoping, that when tested, as I knew I was going to be, that I would prove to be the man my late father Jack, would be proud of. Honest, strong and never arrogant but never a coward. I often hear talk of folk in emotionally testing situations claiming there is nothing they wouldn't do for people special to them. Now was to be my time.

In the early summer of 1998, not long after Dave and John were back from successfully completing the challenge I recall a conversation with Dave in which he said that he had noticed a difference in me from the outset of that event. When pressed he clarified his observation, "You never seemed totally committed to the event this time, as if there was something on your mind."

Dave and I have completed two previous challenges

3

together along with numerous other walking trips, including the French Alps. So, if anyone knew me from an in the hills point of view it was him, and he was correct. I knew even as we left for Scotland, that my marriage of approaching eighteen years was all but over. We had two young sons and I was continually agonising about when to leave. I had lived the terrible results of parents staying together for the sake of the children and was determined not to subject our sons to the sound of continual arguments or the silent tears as they lay upstairs listening to the two people they love and need the most in their innocent worlds, tearing each other to pieces.

If I left though, it would be like severing my limbs because my sons were my very reason for living at that particular point in my life, but I knew I would be back for them. I was convinced I was the better parent and would be more able to bring them up in an open and unbiased environment, but would the courts and various agencies believe me? Could I, a full time employed male really wrest the children from their mother? There were many uncertainties ahead, yet only two things seemed certain.

I was soon to leave my wife. The reasons for that will remain personal, forever, as they are wholly irrelevant to this book which details my journey after leaving the family home, my emotions during the next decade and my outcome.

The second was that I was in for one hell of a series of battles, and those battles were to become the journey. A journey for which I had neither route nor distance, only a hopeful destination.

Sitting in the lounge late one July evening, a mere two months after returning from the ill-fated trip to Scotland, I'd cycled the eight or so miles home after a late shift in the city centre and was watching The Tour de France. An event which as a cyclist I loved and would take every opportunity to escape into. In fact the previous Summer I'd enjoyed a week in the Pyrenees with six like minded individuals cycling the famous mountain passes and watching Le Tour make its swift way through the region.

As I watched on this particular evening I was overcome by a sense of almost calm. I knew this was the time to go. The following morning, whilst at work I decided I had to do this now. I drove home and told my wife I was leaving.

Looking back on the series of events now, as I have done countless times over the years it seems as if it was meant to happen, but I can't really understand why. Several hours after telling my wife I was ending our marriage, I lay on the bedroom floor crying with the boys as I told them of my decision. I still knew I was right even though we were hurting so deep. A depth of conviction comparable only in my life thus far, to the sense of love and utter commitment to them as each were born. I was present at both births and will always hold those moments as the most precious of my life, bar none. I felt pain so sharp that it made the foot infection I suffered earlier that year seem a non-event.

Was this some form of masochistic ritual? So painful, yet

so right. I was to wait a long time for the answer to that question as well as some degree of understanding, but in that moment I just knew I was right to leave and had to hang on to that thought.

Telling the boys was the most difficult thing I have ever done and would ever do in my life. I cried, we cried, we hugged and I promised to come back for them. I'm not sure they fully understood or even, given the circumstances, realised what I had said. They were ten and seven.

This was a moment that was to provide me with much strength and determination over the coming decade. It seems strange to have a moment so utterly sad and innocence shattering as a pivotal moment, to be revisited countless times. Not re-visited to deal with sorrow or guilt but to draw strength and take direction.

In a strange way I drew a similarity from the book 'It's Not About The Bike' by Lance Armstrong, several times Tour de France winner. After his successful battle against testicular cancer he returned to cycling, to go on to multiple tour wins and in doing so recorded some epic mountain stage victories during which he rode with almost superhuman strength and determination leaving other world class cyclists trailing in his wake. As he put it "After suffering and surviving chemotherapy, no mountain road or level of physical pain could ever hurt me again." I knew what he meant.

After telling our sons Lewis and Gavin that I was in effect leaving them, albeit temporarily, I doubt I will ever be afraid to tell anybody anything, or do anything for fear of the consequences again. My heart simply cannot hurt that much again, nor could anything I may have to say ever cause such pain. The look of disbelief and loss in their eyes will live with me forever.

So to continue in the absolute belief that I was right to be doing this, I hope goes some way to explain my depth of feeling in that moment.

Maslow's 'Hierarchy of Needs,' which classifies the various stages of fulfillment we find ourselves in, will probably explain why I left the house with only a cycle, some clothes in a bin bag and a case of red wine! The lowest state of fulfillment is survival. I needed to be able to get to work, clothe myself and maybe the wine was just to null the pain and allow some sleep.

Was I really at the 'survival' stage? I may have thought at that moment that I couldn't get any lower, but oh how wrong was I? Life and the law had so much more in store!

As I lay that first night away from home and the boys, on the floor of a kind friend's bed-less spare room, I still had no feelings of doubt. I had made my decision based on a great deal of thought and some of the forthcoming implications I was able to foresee, others not. Either way I would deal with them. I knew it was right for me, and I believed, it was to be ultimately right for the boys too. Harsh some may think for a father who has just left the two most precious souls he has ever known.

But I firmly 'believed' in the path I was choosing.

HEART BREAKING TIMES

Working in a very public domain, the days drifted by. A uniformed patrolling Police Officer is expected, and quite rightly so, to be there for other folks. To help, to advise and in some cases to make decisions with sometimes life changing consequences.

Spending my working days in such a demanding arena fully occupied my mind and enabled me to remain professional. Yes, of course, there were moments when my own situation would start to occupy my thoughts but always the radio clipped to my chest would spark into life and replace my issues with someone else's.

Away from work I waited for events to occur, not knowing what they were going to be, but always ready to deal whatever, as best I could. Sometimes the waiting was psychologically painful. Not knowing what to expect, if anything.

Not knowing what the boys were thinking was the real problem. I have never really been a worrying sort of bloke, but this not knowing was ripping me to pieces. Weight was falling off me and I was becoming more withdrawn each day.

Several weeks after my bed-less room phase, I had taken up the offer of lodging with another close friend. This time in a room with a bed! I was even starting to get mail, albeit most was from Solicitors or the Child Support Agency but at least in a gallows humour way it convinced me that I was still someone worth writing too.

My world was getting dark, yet with occasional flashes of light. Light so bright and so warming. These flashes were the brief times spent with my two young sons. I longed for these moments even though as any parent in this situation will testify they are over too quickly. I ached for them to spend more time with me, and for me to spend more, much more, time with them.

Two young innocents, who were part of my every fibre, yet were they slowly drifting away from me? This was the point that all parents will understand. When we each look into the eyes of our children, whether babies, toddlers or even bloody annoying teenagers there is a connection. One of trust and utter commitment. Was there distance behind their eyes, or was I just becoming paranoid already?

Typically, one summer morning I stood at the door of my digs waiting for what used to be our car to pull up. It would arrive and the boys would jump out and, not sure whether or not to hug me, would stand nervously alongside whilst my wife, their mother, delivered strict instructions, to me – their father. Details as to when they were to be ready for collection, my instinct was to stand for my rights, as fifty percent of their parents to say when they would be ready and never bow to dictation. However inside these two precious souls, were

9

emotions and feelings of love and loss, of confusion and possibly in this raw nerve arena, even of dislike? These emotions I had to handle with the very highest quality kid gloves. So I bowed to dictation, for now.

Vulnerability was beginning to set in, then the car would be gone. Eight hours of fun was now on the horizon - let's go and try to enjoy the day. All I wanted to do was hold them so close to me that they could never be prised away, but pressure on them in any form was totally wrong. My feelings were much less important than theirs.

After a short walk to the railway station we would wait in anticipation. Nervous answers from them, at my nonstop questions about school, fun things etc. These questions were normal parental questions which are asked daily in the 'normality' of the family home. This situation however was not normal and I was desperate to learn all about what was happening for them and at the same time attempt to show that I am still as devoted as ever to them. I never sought to pry or use them as information sources. A stance I took then and am proud to say have kept until this day, and always will.

The train approached – novel in a macabre way. They were not used to public transport as we had all enjoyed the trappings of a two income family so a trip on the train was indeed a novelty. I on the other hand was getting very familiar with public transport as well as my cycle!

A short journey and the seaside was ours. I was always the dad who got into trouble for keeping them out playing too long, getting them too dirty or even a classic when I took them to play junior rugby before we split and allowed them to drink from my water bottle which contained an energy supplement. I had gone off to work in the afternoon leaving my wife with two already energetic boys whom I had just filled with more fuel!

Playing with them on the beach was second nature to me and indeed to all three of us. We had spent many hours on holiday on the beach, in the sea or just fooling around on the grass. This allowed a degree of normality albeit temporarily into this bizarre situation. Thank goodness I had always been a hands-on dad. Sea, sand, chips, ice cream etc. and not forgetting the train ride back – I'm so the same age as them. We would make our way back on the train and be relaxed in each other's company by the time we were back at my lodgings.

"Mum's here," one of them shouted. In that split second – my heart would be ripped out, completely, without the anaesthetic of realising the time I hadn't prepared myself for their departure. Maybe this was the safest way. If I were to watch the clock my mood would slowly darken and no doubt the boys would feel it too.

At least hugs were now Ok – I could touch them one last time, inhale them, as I used to when they lay as freshly bathed babies on my bare chest. "Don't cry daddy," said the youngest as I hugged them farewell. Without realising it, I was crying again, tears flowing freely down my face. The tear blurred image of a large and comfortable car moving away complete with its precious cargo waving joyfully was my vision till I next

11

saw them. Joyfully, I hoped.

In the space of ten priceless hours I had been optimistic, delighted, but more over I was actively being a dad. Dad was all I wanted to be and all I could be. Sadly the day would end with devastation as they were driven away, but through the tears I had memories. Memories that no one could take away from me, ever.

Later that evening as I completed endless forms for the Child Support Agency, I consoled myself in the knowledge that I wanted to pay maintenance. I wasn't like guys I knew who actually avoided the Child Support Agency or maintenance payments. It still makes my blood boil to hear of parents, bragging about having dodged this, or any other arrangement for paying maintenance. These are our children for God's sake, not something to be avoided like a disease. Would the boys ever understand? Would they ever know? Would they forget my love? Would they forget me? This was no time for self pity but there was so much beginning to torture me, travelling constantly between my head and stomach, both in turn feeling all the worse for each return visit.

Eventually fatigue would take over and lower the curtain. Only to raise it, what seemed just a brief moment later but it was another day and time to start the trip to work.

Cycling fifteen undulating miles twice every day certainly had its benefits. The paunch I had been developing was fast disappearing. This, coupled with a general lack of appetite was turning this portly middle aged guy into his former athletic self.

Cycling was a big part of my life and I regularly rode fifty to sixty miles for fun, and in all weathers. This was perhaps as well as I had left behind a beautiful car. The car however was only an object. For now I was happy to cycle in the knowledge that the car was a little piece of normality still for the boys.

~

Riding home one Friday evening in the wind and rain of an approaching autumn was made enjoyable by the knowledge that early tomorrow I only had to ride twenty five miles to my former home to spend the day with the boys whilst my wife went out for the day. Regular contact with the boys was making me feel as good and happy as circumstances would allow. Obviously there would never be enough time with them but I had to settle for these days and hours, for now. Snippets of time more precious than any jewel.

Morning arrived; it was raining, but not in my mind. I set off with a happy heart and legs so powerful. Up the hill along the flats across the bridge, across the downs I was flying. My new found slender self, coupled with lots of miles on the bike, was certainly paying dividends.

All I could see were the boys smiling, full of fun and ready for a day with dad. I was back in 'dad' mode. What a shame I failed to see the wet tarmac joint in the recently completed roadworks as my trusted racing cycle whooshed across the road surface on tiny areas of rubber.

The pain and shock were pushed aside momentarily as I rolled across the road surface with my helpless stare fixed like radar onto the panicked eyes of the oncoming bus driver. He was almost upright in his cab gripping the wheel and braking so hard I could hear the friction. I have heard of traumatic events described in almost slow motion as the victim recounts the event. Why not me? Why not this? My life, and now I, were spinning and tumbling very fast and out of control. "Please let me get control back, please help me," was all I thought.

I saw my feet, brightly clad in bizarre looking silver cycling shoes, lead the way between the front wheels of the bus, then darkness. An intense heat and the smell of burning brakes engulfed my senses as the bus and I came individually to a standstill with our paths overlapped. My senses were in overdrive. I'm not feeling any pain.

Am I ok? Am I paralysed? Am I alive?

My recollection is that I came to rest with my head between the front wheels and feet under and pointing towards the rear of the bus. It wasn't a big bus, a twenty seat city hopper type but all the same it was much bigger and stronger than I.

After a few moments I crawled out from under the bus, between the front wheels, limped across to the pavement and sat on the grass verge. I had no idea where my bike was, and to be honest not much more idea about where I was!

Then I saw the blooded knees, my knees. My thighs and buttocks had also shed lots of skin, not to mention the lycra shorts. My right hip was now so painful and despite my best efforts to fight it, the nausea and pain took over.

I recall being curled over on the grass verge, retching, but as I had an empty stomach when I left half an hour earlier, I wasn't about to produce anything now. There were people around me but I wasn't sure who, although I assume one was the bus driver. I remember the feel and smell of the grass. I have always, and still do love to walk barefoot on the grass. Without getting too deep here, I suppose it's a 'connecting with the earth' feeling, but for now I was just delighted to be able to feel, smell and retch!

I don't recall much about the intervening moments but eventually and I suppose inevitably I was lying in an ambulance. I gave my details to a police officer who would call my wife and tell her what happened. Today's time with the boys was simply not going to happen. That was the most painful thing. That was what the tears were really for.

Well-meaning comments such as "Ooh that looks sore" and "You will know about this in the morning," were commonplace whilst lying in the hospital's Accident and Emergency department.

After a couple of hours of examination and x-rays, the nurse telling me that nothing was broken seemed so irrelevant. Yes, I was pleased that I was just going to have a few sore days but nothing was going to kill the pain of the realisation that I wasn't going to spend the day with the boys. Not even the handful of painkillers I waddled out of hospital carrying could numb that pain.

Picture this; a shocked, sore and very upset me waiting outside the hospital holding my cycling shoes, a bike with the wheels removed and my arse hanging out of what was left of my shorts. My frustration was growing as I tried to convince the steady flow of taxi drivers that my bike would go in the boot, my dressings were secure, I really have no trousers and NO, I won't stain your car seats!

Eventually a kindly soul accepted my pleas and whisked me the ten or so miles back to my new lodgings.

Once inside I saw there was a message on the answer machine from the police officer who attended the accident. The message;

"We have told your wife yet she seems less than sympathetic. Get well soon mate."

I had anticipated a lack of concern from some, but what were the boys thinking? Not knowing or being allowed to speak to them on the phone was nothing short of agonising. I hadn't intentionally dived off my bike and under a bus, but I accepted that it was my fault. I hadn't been knocked off, I just failed to see the wet tarmac join. Possibly a lack of concentration, maybe my mind was elsewhere. Who is to say but what is done is done and I needed to let myself heal and get to see the boys as soon as possible.

A week or so later and with physical dignity returned it was again time to ring and plead for a day or so with the boys. Following a fairly civil conversation it was agreed that I could spend a day with them. Never under estimate the healing power of happiness. The anticipation of the forthcoming day with the boys had me buoyant both physically and emotionally. I started to use these days as emotional crutches.

As an operational police officer the shift pattern which covered the entire daily cycle, was set for the good and benefit of the community and the force; not to suit my desire to be with my sons. I had to arrange time with them on my rest days which sadly didn't always include the weekends and rarely could I get to see them during the evenings. I knew this, but again craved some confirmation that the boys knew that the reason was that I wasn't able, rather than I didn't want to. The latter was so far from the truth it wouldn't be measurable.

They knew I worked nights and evenings as well as daytime. I just had to hope that they understood too. I had been told on many occasions that children are far more resilient, and understand far more than we give them credit for. I genuinely believe this, and would comfort anyone in a similar position. Provided you are honest with them they will see, believe and ultimately trust you. It may take some time for them to grasp it, and the wait for that confirmation can be agonising, but hang in there.

We would talk and in doing so I hoped their minds were being gently put at ease. I loved these two little guys more than anything, or anyone on this planet because after all, I was a full on dad, no more no less and with a heart so big and full of love.

WHO WILL HEAR MY PLEA?

The first few months after leaving, was an extremely difficult time which seemed to consist of filling in forms way into the night, mostly from the Child Support Agency, but never the less important forms.

The value of which I would benefit from much later in the journey. Again, if you are in a similar position and the relentless invasion and thirst for personal information is getting to you, simply don't give up. Every form you fill in and return, every phone call you answer, every piece of cooperation you show is recorded on some agency computer, and conversely every display of petulance, unreturned form, or refusal to declare your life open for official scrutiny will be similarly recorded.

Anyone who advises you differently is no friend of yours so distance yourself very quickly from this kind of guidance. As I said right at the start of the journey, make sure you are honest with yourself about what you want.

The torrent of forms began to steady to a trickle and contact with the boys started to settle to a vague pattern based around my shifts, mum's commitments and obviously school, or so it was until I started seeing another lady some three months after leaving.

A lady indeed, so dignified and graceful. A lady who showed me warmth and caring of a kind I so desperately craved. Was it on the rebound? Maybe. Was it too soon? Again, maybe. Why was I getting involved in another relationship so soon? Was I feeling something I had long missed? How long would it last? Who knows the answers to all these questions, certainly not me, but for now it felt good. It was too early to tell anything more, but a hidden part of me came alive when I saw her. Her smile as she walked towards me caused warmth within me, and on the outside a strange tautness would pull across my face. I would be smiling again; and it had been a while.

As for how long and how far the relationship with Louise would develop, only the coming months or years would decide. For now she was the medicine I needed, indeed ached for.

Feeling happy gave me the strength to continue in the same determined manner in my quest to secure eventual custody of my little guys. I couldn't run on empty and I am still convinced as I write this that to stay as happy as I could be, for these reasons, was right to try and force away the feelings of guilt which frequently visited me. Life is not a rehearsal.

Once the workplace grapevine gossiped its way through to my friend's wife, the moment for a vicious attack had arrived. There was no earthly reason to have told my wife of my new relationship. I had never offended her so revenge wasn't an issue. She and I had always got along well and I still have no understanding of why she saw fit to dive in and blow everything apart. My new relationship wasn't to be kept secret;

I just would have wanted to tell the boys myself. However, that wasn't to be.

"You bastard, you will never see the boys again and I hope the two of you will be very happy, not."

These words were spat down the phone with venom so deadly I went dizzy. My legs turned to jelly, my heart sank and I felt sick. The conversation was short, not really a conversation in the true sense of the word, but short all the same. A friend whom I had valued in her own right, not just a mate's wife, was the knife that cut the developing thread of contact. My friendship had been repaid with needless poison.

As I lay in bed crying again it was so difficult to console myself in the knowledge that I hadn't engaged in unseemly arguments to try and find out why she had made the call, and therefore still had my dignity intact.

The summer passed, autumn arrived and throughout both seasons a tidal wave of venomous attacks continued through whichever channel was available. Some hurt superficially, others bounced off with little or no effect but others went so deep that even to write this and recount them the pain returns, but only physically now.

The poisonous letters written to the head of the organisation that my friend, and for the moment landlord, worked for, the lies and accusations that he was harbouring an adulterer and child abandoner understandably became too much for a guy only recently divorced himself. He asked that my lady no longer stayed over. So, clearly I had a choice to make. I couldn't stay at his place forever. I'd been there over three months and had accepted that my relationship with Louise was developing well despite all the hatred being fired our way. This was a time to move on.

Louise was living in a friend's spare bedroom, and so was I, so we decided that albeit sooner than we would have wished we looked into renting somewhere together. So it was decided we would share. The house, the costs, everything.

The expected volley of abuse and the threats that I would never see the boys again came and went as I informed my ex-wife of my plans to move into a rented house with Louise.

I now knew oh so clearly that as well as the Child Support Agency issues, I was in for a ding-dong fight in the courts just to see the boys until I was ready to move for anything more permanent. A court system I was to visit regularly over the coming decade, just to gain access to my sons. A court system that despite claims to the contrary is a criminally sad place, filled with a variety of desperate people.

Firstly, estranged parents or guardians so desperate to see their children that they look for, and indeed clinging to any ray of hope. Rays sometimes so obscure they are almost virtual, and when tested usually fall at the first hurdle. Even to describe these hopes is a huge emotional challenge. These rays of hope, if indeed granted, are permitted begrudgingly and at huge financial as well as emotional cost by the second, and far more squalid and uncaring inhabitants of these soulless places; the lawyers.

I had seen many times during my time as a police officer how the lawyers conducted their business with apparent wholesale disregard for personal emotion. I had, however naively let myself be drawn into the hope that in the family court, love and emotion, the very fibres that hold families together, would be the parameters within which all cases would be judged. Hoping that the word and mind games played out at huge expense to the tax-payer, and the varying degrees of torment to all parties involved, would be absent from the family arena. Sadly I was to be proved so wrong.

Please, if you are in a situation similar to mine don't be worried about the acidic tone or verbose language used by the professionals to worry you, and remember that adversary does not mean enemy. Don't think of them as the enemy because if you do, it will cloud the issue by becoming too focused on beating them rather than achieving your goal. The children's welfare is everything.

I had found a decent place to live, three bedrooms and fairly tidy. Room for the boys to visit in the interim before I moved to get full custody. I needed a stable home with sufficient local amenities, shops, schools public transport etc. Where I was now living had just that and I knew I had sufficient evidence to prove I was a suitable and indeed capable parent. I also knew, at the risk of sounding arrogant, that I was in a well-respected profession with an unblemished professional and personal reputation. I didn't need loads of family around me, which was lucky as they were all in the

North of the country!

I fully intended with the support of my employer to bring the boys up myself. They weren't going to be passed between relatives dependent on my shifts. I wish to make the point that I know many thousands of single parents rely hugely on the help and support, in various ways, of family and friends. I'm not for a second criticising this, more making the point that I had a job which allowed great flexibility for single parents. When the time came for me to have full custody I intended to take full advantage of their flexibility so that I could be a more hands on dad.

Love and security are the two most important emotions to wrap young souls in and it matters less how they are bestowed, so long as they are, and that the children are aware. I just now needed to start building up the material possessions. This would take time, but I was fast becoming a master of the car-boot sale price haggle, as well as the scourge of local charity shops and second hand furniture barns.

Alas, long before we actually got to court, evidence of my naivety was beginning to arrive through the letter box. At first a trickle, then a steady flow building to a daily occurrence. Letters that questioned my integrity as a person, a father, my ability to cope and already talking of costs. Costs projected to be so high that I may find them prohibitive in my ultimate quest to gain custody of the boys.

There were many forms of subtle yet individually ineffective threats which, were I allowed to deal with each in its own time, would be laughably pathetic. However, collectively and one after another, like body blows without time to draw a breath between, I was starting to feel weakened.

Louise had two young children, a son and a daughter. Although they were later to live with us, we kept them out of the proceedings, and screened them from all the drama in an attempt to allow them to grow and develop as freely as possible.

As I said, Louise and I had secured a rented family house in a family area and were beginning to get together the beds, wardrobes and raiding charity shops to buy clothes for the boys on their visits. I am not too proud to admit I used charity shops a great deal. The last thing I needed in a custody hearing was large debts. Financial stability was a part of parenting too and I felt I was getting somewhere. I had weathered the storm, for now, maybe.

Picture the scene; a rest day from work, a bit of a lay in. Once up I stumbled, sleepy eyed down the stairs and collected the mail on the way to the kitchen. Almost a scene of British normality. Blah blah Child Support Agency letter, blah blah solicitor letter, both wanting more information so I filled them in and sealed them ready for return.

I had even begun to treat these letters, easily identifiable by their various envelope markings, as my normal daily post. One, however, turned my temporary sunshine to darkness. I opened a letter, not only had I not foreseen but I would never have guessed the content. It was an application to the County

Court to move the boys to live in Berkshire. Over one hundred miles away! My ex-wife's family were going to assist her buy a new house to start a new life. I turned to jelly.

The fear of the boys being ever further away surged through me again. Surging with a power I hadn't felt in a long while. This was a stern reminder that this series of battles was far from over, in fact it had barely started. In court I stood alone, without a state funded legal team. I'm a professional person who earned well and so was there for the taking and not to be given any help. I am certainly not one for self – pity, but I have to say again I feel our country's family legal system is a disgrace.

A pathetic figure in clothes now too big to even nearly fit, I tried with reasoned argument, not to stop the boys being surrounded by the support they would need but to state clearly that with cooperation from their mum we could still provide the clear love and stability they needed to develop. The situation they found themselves in was alien, and beyond their control. Thousands of couples separate but with common sense and the true desire to put personal feelings aside, the children's needs can and must be put first.

Just one honest look into their eyes should be all a parent needs to get the answer as to how we should behave. In my opinion at that time, and to this day, moving them a hundred miles away was a rash, ill conceived decision and wholly wrong. I was now fighting a battle so bloody and all consuming that I had barely time to replenish energy expended daily. I was without car or appetite for food.

I pleaded with the court that, I have no car – I gave it to my wife when I left. Train fares are beyond me for that distance and that regularity. I work shifts, and their mother has clearly stated that although she has a car and sufficient funds she will not assist in helping our children keep regular contact with me, their father.

Whilst I have always fought for what is best for the boys I was now fighting for contact with them and that would keep me going. As well as firmly believing that regular contact with both mum and myself was best for the boys, I worked shifts and simply couldn't get every other weekend off.

I suppose it would have been almost a small victory had my pleas fallen on deaf ears but the truth is the pleas did not even reach the ears that mattered. The judge looked at me with all the compassion of an executioner and granted my ex-wife all she and her team had asked for.

It was as if I'd been silenced, the judge could see my mouth moving but no sound arriving at her ears. A father asking for assistance, how dare he?

How can a legal system that allows a parent to blatantly state in court that she is not prepared to assist in contact arrangements for the benefit of the children, feel anything other than shame.

I had just reached a new low in Maslow's Hierarchy of Needs. This was now fighting for survival. I felt very much alone and legally unrepresented. I was an honest, loving, hard-working dad in a family court. This is what real alone is.

I had never realised that the Child Support Agency had a direct link to the County Court system, or was this next body blow a cruel irony! The very next day the Child Support Agency assessment arrived and I felt sick as I read it, repeatedly. Nearly one thousand pounds upfront and several hundred pounds per month. It was so dismissive of my earlier efforts to pay maintenance from the day I left.

As I mentioned earlier I am not and have never been a maintenance dodger. I left in July and this assessment arrived in October. I had already made enquiries with solicitors to see what a fair sum was to pay monthly and did so. But to my horror the Child Support Agency refused to recognise I had paid anything in those interim three months, which coincidentally was just short of the sum they wanted up front. That demand could only be waived with the cooperation and confirmation of the other party. That wasn't about to happen, despite my pleading.

It's no wonder really that some parents feel the need to withhold payment of any maintenance until the Child Support Agency get round to completing their assessment. The sheer stupidity of rules that ignore genuine well meant payments, unless the receiving party confirms this defies belief.

I suppose that my desire to support the boys from day one, that mental contract I entered into the second they were born, was about to cost me but they would always know that I put them first on this and every other occasion. If reading this you are in a similar situation, the dilemma is one for you to fathom out. I can't offer guidance other than to say the decision you eventually make is one you may have to wait many years to find out whether it was the right one. Eventually the children become adults and they will want to know the truth. Secondly, there is always the possibility that they may end up in the same situation. Ask yourself this; have I demonstrated unconditional love and support for them in such a way as they may continue to love and respect me and my values as they grow, or have I allowed money and a desire to score points by exercising a perverse financial control over the other parent to become more important to me? It really is your call.

All I could see in my mind was the boys. I really didn't give a shit about money. Never have done, never will do. The harsh facts though were that I needed money now, to travel four hundred miles twice a month to get the boys and then take them home. I missed them so very deeply they were and still are, the very centre of my reason for living.

GAINING NORMALITY

Over the following months I spent many hours musing over bank statements which were proving that I simply couldn't afford the train fares to see my sons. Eight return tickets twice a month was almost two hundred pounds in total. Remember this was in the late nineties and fares were a few percent less but still very expensive!

I suppose it was at this stage that I got into a dark and dangerous routine of continually taking body blows without retaliation and I tried desperately not to let the boys see me angry, despite my inner rage. I tried also to show them that I missed and loved them dearly but never to show my deepening hatred of the system that I felt was allowing them to be used to hurt me. The system indirectly caused them huge amounts of pain that would take far longer to heal. Where was the focus on the children?

I didn't hate their mother then, nor since, nor even now. My hatred was for a system that allows and indeed blindly supports such one sided behaviour. I wish to make it clear that I'm not an advocate of any organisations that fight solely for father's rights, each case is individual and should be treated so.

I accept many publicity stunts you hear of in the news are

desperate attempts of fathers who have probably tried all other means just to have an equal say in bringing up the children they deeply love. After all I am one of them. I am, however, of the school of thought that the emotion felt by all parents in these painful times, if channeled through a path of reasoned but robust legal argument will be far more effective in the long run, and to the good and benefit of all, especially the children. Used like a crowbar to open doors sealed with laws so old as to bear little relevance to today's society, and hopefully to bring about change in the law.

A change that just gives both parents equal footing in court surely can't be that difficult, but as I have said and will undoubtedly repeat, it's a matter of willingness and co-operation.

Waiting in the car park at Reading station I cut a forlorn figure. Several months had passed and the inevitable move to Berkshire had taken place.

Sometimes they would arrive in an aunt's car, sometimes never arrive at all. When people, family or otherwise, who are involved in or close to the situation elect to show their allegiance or feelings, some of the sources of support can be very surprising.

I am and will always be grateful for the ability and willingness of the boys' aunt to put aside personal feelings and indeed family loyalty to bring the boys to the railway station to meet me.

I have no doubt, given comments made in an earlier court

session, that without her help I would not have been able to see the boys on any regular basis at all. Whilst I must admit to an initial degree of suspicion as to her motives, it was soon clear from the boys' comments and lack of investigative questions that her concern was only for the boys. I had gained a deep respect for their aunt and indeed was to develop a bond of trust over the ensuing years based on a genuine desire to see the boys grow and develop in a balanced manner.

When they arrived all was forgotten for forty eight hours. Running through the station to the train, I would now be surging with positive energy. Once on the train I was a dad again, non-stop conversation for an hour as I sought to satisfy my thirst for knowledge about school, scouts, in fact, any facet of their lives, always remembering not to quiz them for information. The last thing I wanted was for them to think I was using them for information about their mum. They should be free to talk, to express feelings and to love me and their mum as we, now independently, love them.

Once home, Louise would meet us at the station and my weekend would really begin.

Their presence simply made my weekend. Without them it was a very dark place no matter what day of the week. I dearly hoped that being with me made their weekend special too.

We played, talked about things, anything they wanted and we even planned a holiday. They and I always had a love of the great outdoors. Family holidays were primarily of the camping type in France, Italy and many places within the UK. We decided that as it was now summer we would try to get away during the October half term. It was so exciting to book flights on the web, look at maps and plan our adventure. We were to fly to Scotland, stay in a walkers' hostel and then mountain bike till we dropped. Things they loved to do when their mum and dad still loved each other.

These are the times I clung to. A few stolen hours twice a month became almost normal. From the tearful farewells at the end of each weekend I would be focused on, and living purely for the next "Hello."

Alternatively, should they not arrive at the station, the minutes and then the hours would tick by and the sickening realisation would set in that I would not be seeing them that weekend.

I would wonder how they were feeling?

Were they as sad and disappointed as I was?

Were they missing me?

Was this self-pity?

Was it parental concern or just a potent combination of emotions, called love?

The next move was obvious, without the boys. I would make my way to the station bar and although it never really helped, on these occasions I just did it. I would buy a bottle of wine and drink till the train arrived, then take the rest with me to finish on the awful journey home without them.

I suppose I was fortunate in my love of wine because a fiver would buy a decent bottle of red which contained more anaesthetic than two pints of Guinness, and it lasted longer. I know that no cure was ever found in the bottom of a glass but maybe that saying could be altered to include "no permanent cure."

The relief would quell my desire to go to her house, insist on seeing the boys and risk being arrested. For how long, and how often, could I continue to take these blows?

At these moments I genuinely had no idea. When I get custody, I vowed, I will never treat them or even their mum like this. I will always encourage contact with both parents and respective families. I will get custody, I refuse to contemplate failure.

In the summer of 1999, with great help and the continuing calming influence of their Aunt Pam, the contact became more regular and less of a lottery as to whether they would be allowed to visit me.

We would sit outside and talk in more detail about going on holiday together, just the three of us.

Money was always short but with planning I could afford the budget airline trip we had been discussing to Scotland for a bit of fresh air, mountain biking and above all, togetherness.

I knew how the idea of the boys enjoying time away with me would not go down well with their mum. So I decided to now use the court system to the boys' advantage, and mine too. I decided to apply to the court, the same courts that had inflicted so much hurt on me only a year ago, and ask for an order to allow me to take the boys to Scotland.

A reasonable request. I was able to explain in detail our plans for travel, accommodation and activities whilst there. The secret here was to only make a reasonable request.

I decided to start getting a record of responsible parenting and use the courts to keep that record. I may in the future have to show that I can be a full–time dad. Armed with that order, ironically unopposed, permitting me to take them out of the country I booked the flights from Stansted to Glasgow, a hire car for a few days and even a hotel near Stansted the night before we flew.

Once in Scotland we would drive north to Newtonmore. It's a beautiful area in the Speyside region about forty miles south of Inverness and very close to the Cairngorm Mountains. We would stay in the same hostel as I had done a little over year before with my foot infection.

I showed the boys all the documents as we pored over various maps for weeks before we were due to go. They were nine and eleven now so I'd hired bikes for them too. I was finally beginning to feel like a normal dad, making decisions and plans with them.

Materially, which I am not as it goes, I was beginning to get together the bits and pieces I would need to allow us all a degree of comfort. I had even bought a small car. It was a Rover 214, with plenty of miles already on the clock. It was a simple, uncomplicated car with the reputation of going on forever, just what I needed.

STAYING FOCUSED

Now I am not without a degree of intelligence, although that is one aspect of my character I have been accused of keeping well hidden, but mechanically I am a total void.

With the possibility of running repairs being so expensive and without the knowledge to argue the bill, I thought the simpler the car I buy the more chance of being able to carry them out myself!

When choosing a car, one of my criteria was that when I lift the bonnet, if I can see the road underneath then there can't be that much there in the first place! Thus leading me to believe there was less that could go wrong.

You mechanical types may scoff at this reasoning, but mark my words, there is logic in it. This car was yet another step in my rehabilitation and was to become a legend.

Following the purchase of my new car, I walked home from the dealers on a brisk September day and decided to stop for a pint. Just the one!

I was enjoying a day off in the week and had a few other chores to attend to. After being true to my word and just having the one with a bit of lunch I arrived home in the early afternoon and decided I would benefit from a haircut too.

So, this fine day plus my positive demeanour coupled with my love of cycling soon had me spinning briskly through the town towards the barbers. The feeling of freedom was increased by the wind in my hair. I had not worn my cycling helmet, as is my habit when going for a haircut as I hate it when those little bits of hair are left behind, (you know the ones guys - the buggers that get so far down your shirt collar that they make your ass itch within minutes of leaving the barbers).

Nearing the barbers I could see there was a queue, stretching out of the shop with four or five guys standing waiting, at least an hour wait, I figured.

Bugger, queuing on a day like this, I decided to go for a nice long ride, a good thirty miles plus. I had, albeit reluctantly, lost a lot of weight and hither to without a car was riding well over a hundred miles a week which had greatly improved my fitness, which perversely was contributing to my general feeling of well-being.

Off I went, I set about the scenic South Gloucestershire countryside full of power in my legs and positive thoughts in my head based on my recent car purchase and the travel opportunities as well as travel convenience that would now open up for me and the boys.

By chance as I made my way out of town and towards my favourite cycling areas I passed two work colleagues, I smiled and waved, they gestured without smiling. I think it was the fact that I had the day off and they didn't. I was cycling through the balmy late summer air while, they were sat in a police

36

patrol car. At least it was the one with air-con!

I was so excited about my car being ready before the coming weekend which was in fact to be the last with the boys before we went to Scotland two weeks later. No more trains! I can't even begin to explain how owning a car again was making me feel. The ability to adjust with flexibility.

During our weekends together we could go out if we wanted to. No longer dependant on public transport or lifts from Louise, who also had busy weekends.

The boys would be so surprised to get picked up in my car before we went shopping for our holiday and I couldn't wait to see them.

Life was as good as I could expect at that moment and I was determined to focus on the positive.

Over the hill and down through the village I sped, on such a classy racing cycle powered by turbo-charged thighs. Fifty mph down the hill must be possible. Head down, arse up and peddling like I was being filmed! Fifty, yes fifty one and fifty two, I peddled as hard and fast as I could.

Even the car behind was hanging back, I decided, in admiration or disbelief at the bright yellow and black lycra-clad vision in front, travelling at such a speed. I was pleased the car didn't try to pass me. Some drivers care nothing for cyclists and a nudge at that speed could have been fatal. This driver however was patient and polite. Once I reached the bottom of the hill the village leveled out and my attempt at the land speed record was over for this trip.

Grateful for the driver's patience I turned my head and shoulders to give him a quick thumbs up as a thank you prior to moving in to let him pass me. Had I not turned to say "thank you" I may have seen the approach of the gently curving kerb. Curving towards me, fast!

I knew I had parted company with my bike. Almost slow-motion like, I also knew I was going to land very soon, and it would be painful!

As I lay on the roadside staring up as if through a long cardboard tube I could see tiny heads with faces looking down at me. I could hear a man on a phone calling an ambulance. I knew he was telling them we were in a village but he was telling them the wrong village. He was in fact sending them in the opposite direction.

I couldn't speak to correct him nor could I move, but I felt no pain. I couldn't even twitch or blink my eyes. All seemed quiet, as if I was in a separate dimension. I could hear all the normal things going on around but with a soft, almost padded effect.

I was suddenly aware of being punched in the throat by a lady who was shouting "He's dead, oh my god he's dead."

No pulse "Who is he, who do we tell?"

By now, and I had no idea of the time-scale, I was aware of quite a crowd around me and I had worked out that I had crashed my bike in some style. I knew roughly where I was. Enough to know that the guy had told the ambulance service the wrong location.

Then it went totally dark.

Not alas physical shutting down or survival plan by the ingenious thing which is the human brain, nor was it me slipping from this life. It was in fact the result of this lady throwing the shittiest, smelliest horse blanket imaginable over me as I lay in the road.

Still unable to move or communicate in any manner I could do nothing to shift this thing. I did decide however, that if I was dying whoever threw this infested thing over me was so going to get haunted. I'd be back!

She was still sitting or kneeling next to me sobbing. Phrases such as "so young" and "what a waste" etc. Gratifying as it was, I would have happily swapped all these maybe posthumous compliments for the removal of this shite infested rag.

Suddenly I could hear a sound very familiar and on this occasion comforting, I could hear the two tone horns of an ambulance. Without going into detail, as a member of the emergency services I could tell the difference between the horns of each of the emergency vehicles.

Sadly these sounds were getting fainter as the ambulance made all haste in the wrong direction.

I knew he'd told them the wrong village!

As one set of horns faded I could pick out another set, slightly different. These however were police horns. I should know, I have driven many frantic miles over the years with these as background music.

Nearer and nearer until at last I heard the vehicle stop close by and the horns switched off.

"F*****g hell it's Reeder." Four words I will treasure. The 'er' bit in 'Reeder' is a Bristolian way of adapting short surnames to form a nickname. If I could hear this then all was not lost. I knew the voice too, one of my colleagues I had joked with an hour earlier. It was Eddie.

Worrying me more was why were the police there? I don't think the car hit me. Was it really serious, or likely to be fatal? I just didn't know.

What the hell is happening to me? As I lay there without the option of movement it was starting to dawn on me that I may just be dying.

My senses were heightened, especially smell. My hearing was acute and registering that the third set of two tone horns I could hear was an ambulance and hopefully as it was getting louder it was coming towards me.

I heard somebody else, I presumed on a phone, saying he is in Charfield and not Wickwar. I tried to take the positive in that if I could hear the conversation, and the horns, I am still me; and not yet just a body!

I began to cry but without tears or movement. I have so much to do yet, so much to give. So much love, so much caring. I simply had to survive to get the boys safe and to see them grow up. I wasn't prepared to contemplate death or leaving them behind.

I cannot go without saying goodbye to Louise, which

would be very wrong. Then the deafening silence as the ambulance horns that had steadily neared us were switched off.

Daylight again, and fresh air as the paramedic lifted the blanket off me. The owner of which I was still planning to haunt!

"He's not dead," said a different voice, "and I've got a pulse."

"I know you have love, but what about me?" I thought to myself, still trying to find humour.

I also felt a strange mixture of anger and frustration. Am I dying or not, make your bloody minds up – I still had no pain. Looking up through my now familiar tube, I saw a paramedic that I had worked with the day before. We had been dealing with a road accident involving a lady who had been knocked off her horse and broken her leg. I watched in admiration as he wielded his scissors clean through her new riding boots, much to her annoyance.

Now I'm no rocket scientist but when I saw him produce the same scissors from his top pocket I began a process of elimination. My shoes were specialist cycling shoes and only had three Velcro idiot fasteners so would not need cutting off. I had no helmet on, so there were no straps to cut. All that remained were my bright yellow and black cycling shirt and shorts. I fail to see why he had to cut these from right thigh to left shoulder. They were so tight that there was nothing that couldn't be seen anyway.

What the hell, why should I worry about dignity when I

am in this state and yet still no pain. After what seemed an age and much prodding it was decided to move me to the ambulance. Now the pain arrived.

I am not really sure where hurt most. My whole being was racked with pain, so deep I wanted to vomit. There was pressure from the spinal board against my pelvis, shoulder and head and pressure from the strap across my forehead holding my head firmly in place.

To this day I couldn't say which spot hurt most. Each source of pain an individual contributory, feeding one main outlet of agony. The injuries? I wasn't really sure at this stage.

I did however feel I potentially had a sight problem. I remember the medics asking the police to return my bike (which was only scratched!) to my home.

When Eddie asked if anyone had picked up the right removable lens from my sunglasses, because he had the left lens and frame in his hands, the male medic stated it was still in my eye. Underneath my eyelid!

Blind in one eye, that may explain the tube vision but not something I relished the thought of. I suppose selfishly I had now settled to the idea that I wasn't to die and therefore any injuries would mend. Life-long effects were definitely not part of my plan.

I later saw on TV that the tube vision I had experienced was a fairly common near death experience!

After a short journey to the trauma wing I was wired, plugged and dripped up to the max. I seemed to be waiting forever to go to x-ray, they planned to scan my entire body before releasing me from the spinal board.

Anyway that was done in the trauma wing. My hopes that the spinal board would be removed so I could be taken to x-ray were dashed. A simple waft over me from toe to head and back to toe by a frame supporting a 'DVD player' sized box, which I took to be the camera, and that was it.

I recall feeling very sleepy, maybe it was the painkillers, or the shock. Maybe a combination, but I was terrified of going to sleep. I think I was now satisfied that I was badly injured, possibly blinded in one eye when this lens is finally removed!

If I go to sleep will I slip back? It was a terrifying thought, but thankfully one I didn't need to dwell long on. Soon a Doctor and nurse, as I recall, began removing the lens from my right eye I and wished I was in the deepest sleep possible.

After a brief look at the x-rays a doctor informed me that the spinal board could be removed. As it did, the pain levels steadily rose as my limbs and muscles had to begin supporting themselves again. The pain this time was just too much. I vomited on the pillow. What a bloody mess to get myself into.

Meanwhile, my colleague Tony had arrived to say he'd taken my bike home and Louise would be down soon. I had, over the previous months allowed our relationship to slip a little. I suppose the popular way of describing it would be to say we were having a rough patch.

The truth is that I was having a rough patch and Louise was desperately trying to understand my mood swings.

Although never aggressive towards her I was becoming single minded in my pursuit of the boys and as always, in any battle there is collateral damage. We were becoming that damage.

Yet here I was, destined to be utterly helpless for a few days and going to have to depend on her kindness when I had no real right to expect it. For now though, as there are no sheep, I'll just lay here and count the tubes coming out of me to help me sleep!

Why is it that when even by not speaking, the facial expressions of people trying desperately to have a conversation with you give away the fact that you look a mess!

A hairline fracture of my scull just above my forehead into my hairline and a thumb nail sized piece chipped out of my pelvis. According to the nurse, now cleaning me up, I had an ass big enough for the piece of pelvis to be lost forever. How lucky am I? Oh and not to forget, I had three broken ribs too. She handed me a small cellophane bag which contained, my glasses lens. It had gone into my eye flat so not cutting me and no complications expected when the elephant man style swelling went down. Genuinely very lucky.

No visible skin on the right side of my face coupled with a grotesquely swollen eye. That will teach me to use my face as a brake.

Right thigh skinless and right knee cut and stitched.

All in all just about ready for the cover of 'Mens Health!'

The final ironic twist, after what seemed an age in the hospital, the clean up was all but complete. "You can go home,"

I was told cheerfully. On the proviso that I get complete rest. Like I could do anything else! Even signing the discharge papers was bloody agony.

"Ok, get yourself dressed and pop back onto the bed I will call your partner to come and get you," said the cheery but efficient nurse, and whoosh she was gone.

I should never really have had a moments doubt because Louise arrived with a warm but concerned smile. I knew instantly that despite the coolness of our relationship at this time, she would do all she could to help me.

"Get dressed," was the nurse's next cheerily delivered command.

"What into," was my immediate reply?

The cut and torn rags in those hospital bags were my clothes before 'captain scissor – hands' turned up. I explained my clothing predicament to the nurse and that Louise had no reason to know I needed clothes to get home.

"Ok no problem," whoosh the nurse was gone again in a flash.

She returned with two paper operating gowns. Yes, you know the ones. As if being poorly was not enough, they make you walk to the car park with your arse hanging out.

No wheelchair, because if I couldn't walk then I couldn't go home.

Shuffle, laugh, cough – shuffle, laugh and cough all the way to the car. At least I could walk, and it served as a reminder that I was indeed lucky enough to be able to.

A couple of weeks later and after several phone calls to those kind enough to give their details to the police at the time of the accident, I had pieced together what actually happened.

Grateful to the motorist for staying back from me whilst hurtling down Charfield Hill who I turned to give a thumbs up. At this I drifted towards the kerb my front wheel hit it. I went over the handlebars and slid along and across a driveway on my face and front. That accounts for the lack of skin, cut knee and glasses lens in the eye.

Then I hit a driveway wall head on, thus accounting for the skull injury. Momentum then flipped me upwards, head on the floor, legs in the air and my back going up the wall and hips bending the wrong way over the wall, which fairly well accounts for the pelvis damage.

According to the elderly lady tending her garden in the autumn sun, I didn't completely go over the wall but dropped down on the side I had arrived on. I stood up, tried to walk but passed out and fell over again.

After she and other onlookers had made various telephone calls the overriding feeling was, "he's a goner!"

I sure am lucky to be here.

EMPTY SEATS

Whilst recovering from my injuries, and desperate to see the boys I drove, possibly unwisely, a week or so later in my 'new' car to Berkshire to get them for the weekend. This was to be the last weekend contact before our trip to Scotland and nothing was going to get in the way of final preparations.

I drove directly to their aunt's house as I could now save the boys from the tawdry spectacle of being handed over in a public place, but I was totally unaware that my wife was there too. Although she had bought a home a few miles away she had clearly stated that she did not want me anywhere near there.

I don't know why and didn't really care so using her aunts home was fine with me. I pulled up at the house and the boys ran out, big hugs and they then jumped into the car.

My ex-wife came out, not to repeat the "Back by seven on Sunday or it's court," warning.

Which to be honest was getting rather tiresome by now as I always took them back in time for bed when it would be school the next day.

But instead I felt to look at and enjoy my injuries. She as a nurse would well know the pain I was in and was not about to miss this vision!

Obviously a short argument ensued which was par for the course. My instinct was to turn and walk away, towards the car, smiling at the boys.

I was as excited to see them as I hoped they were to see me. After no more than a pace or two I felt a sharp tug on my left arm. I turned to clearly say I was not interested in arguing, especially in front of the boys. Nor was I prepared to let our situation become a public spectacle.

Jesus Christ! The pain!

I never saw her left hand on its way. She was left handed, and I was only just getting clear vision back in my right eye. It connected fair and square on my right cheek and, I guess, it was her thumb that went into my eye.

I heard her aunt shout as I stumbled blindly forward.

"Stop it, there's no need for that, get back in the house."

Then, in unmistakable tones, "He deserved it, the bastard."

Sick with shock and pain I quickly got into the car and drove off, the boys silent. Eventually I began, as so often over the coming years, to defend her actions. I don't know why. "Mums just angry guys," I said to them. Let's forget that and think about the good stuff.

"That is what mum calls you all the time, you are even in her phone book under B." The slightly trembling voice of my younger son, as he fought with the dilemma of whether to tell me or not.

Having just seen something so horrific to them, they were battling with love, devotion and loyalty. Exactly the situation I tried desperately to prevent them having to experience, but as I said earlier I had no control over mum's rules.

Ninety minutes or so later we were home. A weekend of excitement, laughing at my injuries and mimicking my walk etc. Looking at the maps of where we would be in two weeks' time. Shopping, food, things to do, who sits near the window on the plane going out and who sits near the window coming back. Seems I was not actually in the draw for that one. Who sits in the front of the hire car?

"Hey, me all the time, I'm driving,"

"You're not funny dad" would be the curt response.

Shopping for warm clothes was great fun, it added to the sense of adventure.

As I sit writing this it is early October and it was about this time of year in 1999 we were preparing for the trip, I am conscious of a soft smile breaking across my face as I recall quite clearly the events of that weekend.

The bright autumn sun, a hint of cold and leaves starting to fall, and in Scotland it would be a few degrees cooler, so that is what we were preparing for. The whole weekend was about the excited planning for that trip.

The internet, absurdly, was in its infancy as we sat and waited for slow, fractured images of the airline, the hostel we were staying in and the snowcapped Cairngorm Mountains that were to be our playground.

Sunday, on time, I dropped the boys off at home, or to be more accurate at the end of the close. Dropping them off at the end of the close was Ok because I didn't have to approach the house, but I insisted on waiting in such a position as to be able to see them go into the house.

I hated beyond belief leaving them at the end of a weekend and my heart ached for the time when I would have custody and although I would always encourage contact with their mum, I would relish the full time responsibility of bringing them up. Boys to men.

The motorway towards Bristol was a quiet, almost calm place for the journey home as I drove with images of their excited faces next time I was to see them.

The interim two weeks I spent healing further and making final preparations.

Time eventually came around to the night shifts, and only a week away till the holiday. I enjoyed nights. Having completed my final night shift it was time to clear the ever increasing pile of paperwork, I'd spent the week looking forward to seven am Friday morning and walking out and away for six days.

The time came and I was feeling tired but good at the prospect of a whole week's leave and most of it with the boys. I was buoyed by a phone call to my wife the evening before to check and confirm I would collect the boys at four from their after school club. Her aunt would meet me and show me where it was. Then to Stansted for the adventure to begin.

I could feel in her voice utter frustration at not being able to thwart this trip.

So, collect at four pm, Travel Inn at Stansted by six, after tea we would chill with a little bit of TV and then early to bed to rise in plenty of time for our morning flight. My mind was spinning with every last detail. After a final check of my alarm I was in bed and swiftly fell asleep full of anticipation. Strange though it was, I never had a problem sleeping.

Before I left, I called their aunt Pam who explained where the club was. I had a reasonable idea so arranged to meet her there. She had to collect the boys as the staff didn't know me. I understood, and set off back up the motorway towards London which was busy, as always on a Friday so I was kept occupied with the driving rather than my mind wandering.

The look on their aunts face as I pulled into the after school club car park spoke volumes, that combined with the fact that there were no cars in the car park. It was shut and had been so all week. Their aunt had been to the house without luck and even spoke to neighbours. The boys and mum had not been seen for a few days.

"They've gone away." one neighbour told their aunt.

I went from summit to dungeon. Descending on an express lift from a summit of elation and anticipation to the dark, dank dungeon of despair.

So sick with worry, trying to assure their aunt whilst at the same time struggling to prevent myself from retching. My stomach was in knots. Where were they? What had they been told? Could I be forgiven a touch of paranoia?

Had the boys been told that I (the B) was not coming after

all? I had this horrendous vision of the boys eagerly waiting the trip, only to be told that I wasn't taking them. So she took them instead.

I still have no understanding of her motive for this, other than purely using the boys to hurt me. I tried desperately not to believe this but it was hard, very hard.

It gets dark fairly early in mid October and it was very dark by mid evening when I eventually accepted, after many hours sitting, waiting and watching for any signs of life at their house, that they were not coming home.

The trip was off for them but I still had a dilemma, do I go or do I stay. I was devastated. Sick with worry but I decided to go.

At least that way I could be alone, to think and to cry if needed as I felt sure I would.

If I went home I would only ruin Louise's weekend and simply couldn't face being my normal fairly buoyant self. Ironically, I was later to find out their mum had taken them to friends in Northumbria, not a million miles away from our intended destination and I probably even flew over them.

I knew she wouldn't hurt them but what was going on in their minds? This was a question for which I had no answer.

The route to Stansted Airport, a combination of three motorways all looked the same through a windscreen of tears. The wipers were hopelessly inadequate. They don't work on the inside. I arrived at the Travel Inn and tried to ignore the bemused look of the receptionist. One bloke, family room –

how does that work?

I had obviously booked a family room and it clearly stated three persons on the reservation. I prayed that she wouldn't enquire further as to why I was alone. She didn't, possibly seeing my red eyes and drawing her own conclusions and, whatever they were, they were Ok by me. It saved me the torture of having to explain.

I repeatedly questioned myself. Shall I still go? Has my ex-wife got the day wrong by just one day? No, they all knew the day, their aunt was proof of that.

I decided to go. Back to the car to rearrange the packing, this was now a trip for one. They clearly weren't allowed to be anywhere near me, for now at least.

I kept telling myself to note it all down and use it effectively, in court if need be, but don't do anything rash. I was now a wounded animal and rightly or wrongly I was ready to lash out, and the blows would be so full of venom and fury that my whole case would never recover credibility.

This feeling worried me. I had never lost control before and simply couldn't afford to now.

I drove to the airport, all of ten minutes and after parking started making my way to the terminal and ultimately to check in. I was trying continually to focus my emotions on getting home and setting the custody ball rolling, for all the right reasons I desperately wanted to be a full time dad.

But all I could do for now was join the inevitably long queue at check-in for my flight. For once in my life how I longed for there to be just two more people in front of me, and another two, and another two. I was desperate to avoid the inevitable questions of the check in staff, as I got nearer and nearer. Eventually I was at the desk and this time they didn't spare my feelings. No I didn't want a refund, I didn't even ask for one, not now, nor after I had travelled, never.

I had only one bag so I wasn't there for long once the inquisition had ended. I could feel the impatience of those behind me; how can he be so long with only one bag? Seven in the morning and I'm sweating already.

Eventually the flight was called and after a cooling walk I climbed the steps to the front entrance of the plane and tried manfully to return the welcoming smile of the air hostess.

I sat down immediately, in one of the three seats on the front row, right next to the front door so I could make best use of the fresh air till the door was closed, and hopefully to be first off when we landed.

I stared blankly out of the window as the aircraft devoured an unending line of people. I prayed for someone to sit next to me, whoever it may be would be no substitute but at least I wouldn't feel so alone.

Eventually, a polite "excuse me sir" coupled with a gentle touch on the shoulder got my attention, it was the air hostess.

Next to her, the kindly face of an elderly lady stared at me. Unwittingly she was about to drive a dagger deep into my heart. So unfair for a lady who looked as if she had never had a malicious thought in her life.

She spoke softly, and before the air hostess could utter another word,

"Is anyone sitting here," as she gestured to the two vacant seats next to me.

"No," I said quietly with a resigned shake of my head, and offering as welcoming a smile as I could.

By mid afternoon the flight had been just a flight. I collected my hire car and drove lots of miles into and through the steadily changing scenery. From lush green pasture land eventually to tree-less heather clad mountains.

These hills have been and always will be a source of inspiration as well as perspective for me.

I had found for myself, a place which allows me the space to calmly think and plan.

Eventually I pulled into one of my favourite places; Newtonmore, a small Highland village about twelve miles south of Aviemore, between the Cairngorm and Monahdliath Mountain ranges. It's a real gem.

It was to become a very important place for me. A place of safety, a place to recover and recharge.

A place to plan.

QUIET THOUGHT

Getting out of the car in the now dark Highland evening, Kathryn from Newtonmore Independent Hostels met me on the crunchy gravel car park.

A bemused smile shot across her face as she tried to be discreet whilst looking behind me into the obviously empty car.

I just knew that following the delightfully clipped accent saying,

"Halloo again Geoff," was soon to follow an enquiry as to the boys' whereabouts.

"Have ye no got the bairns?" No sooner had she asked, than I strode into the rays of the security light and she could see instantly what had happened from the expression on my face. The kindly hug and offer of a cup of tea was so very welcome. I was shaking with sadness and even though I wanted to cry, I didn't need to.

The following few days I put myself through some gruelling hill walking, not only was I physically getting over the crash but I seemed to be more capable of quiet thought.

I seemed to be gaining the ability to think along one train of thought without other random issues diving in to disrupt me.

Navigating over the Scottish hills in the on-setting winter

was no place for getting mentally side-tracked, no matter what the issues. Then in the evenings in the quiet of the hostel I could lie with my notes, adding to them as I gradually formulated my plan.

Like a jigsaw, my plan would have to be resilient, calm, accurate and above all filled with care. Not passionate aggression that could be destructive. I needed, and indeed had to make good use of my quiet thought time. Professionals may have a more specific term for this but 'quiet thought' is my way of understanding and explaining it.

What was really happening, again unclear to me at the time was that my own position in the developing custody and contact conflict was getting even stronger. This horrendous episode of denying the boys a holiday and more importantly contact with their other loving parent was ultimately to be looked on very gravely by the courts and social services.

These very agencies, without my initiation, were beginning to take concerned notice of the treatment to which the boys were being subjected.

As already mentioned, support can come from very surprising quarters. There may well be some initial suspicion, but allow it in gently and under scrutiny. Analyse the reasons for the support, but never knock it away if it's genuinely for the benefit of the children.

A potential ally is priceless, once in your camp they can't return to the other side. If they have the children's best interests at heart then reel them in and keep them close.

I arrived home a few days later and began to enquire as to why the boys had been taken away. This proved to be very difficult. Mainly because I couldn't get through by phone nor was I being allowed normal parental rights of information from the schools. The web of lies and deceit being spun to block my every route to the boys was seemingly impregnable.

Lewis' secondary school were under the impression that there was a court order preventing me accessing the boys and preventing the school discussing progress and welfare with me. The same was happening at the junior school.

Even the boys' friends' parents were under the impression that there were orders preventing contact with me at any time.

As I mentioned earlier, these blocks however frustrating I knew would ultimately work for me. You already know my profession so when I say the words "witnesses" maybe you begin to see my evolving plan. I was extremely surprised at the calmness and clarity of thought I was able to display to myself at each stomach wrenching setback. I slowly set about dismantling this web of lies. It wasn't easy.

If there is a court order in existence then it must be delivered to each interested party. I hadn't had one sent nor did I know of any such court application. Each order has to be applied for and with reasons. The process demands that the applicant state on the application who should be precluded from contact and why.

That person, the respondent, as is clear by the title has the opportunity to attend court and put their case in argument. A judge, usually in business suit and in a courtroom no bigger than a large lounge will decide whether to grant the order on the merits of each argument.

Now, as a police officer and not fazed by courts, I always attended these hearings myself.

I appreciate that there may be some folk who don't have that confidence. Please don't think for one second that your love is any less valid. Get a solicitor to put your case for you. Just remember that it is your argument and they are simply your legal guidance and mouthpiece. Don't for one second let them dictate your feelings or ultimate aim.

I made an appointment with the head of year at the relevant schools to see either the court orders or my sons. This is where momentum is so important. Once you gain it don't give it up cheaply.

I knew that they, the school, would have to franticly call their mum and ask for a copy of the order, which of course didn't exist. So I would insist on my rights as a parent to see my sons and be kept informed of their progress.

I think I scared the head of one of the schools so much I was still getting newsletters for years after he left school and was married. Still, I loved my boys and my Mr Quiet, but threatening impression was well worth it!

Threatening is a word that I think needs some explaining. It will do you no good whatsoever to threaten violence, even though, in some circumstances it would be so very easy to deliver. Only threaten what you can deliver in the way of making them answer to the courts for denying you your rights as a parent.

This is a time when you will have to ask them which court granted the order, then check with the court. Once you are sure, be strong. If at any time you feel weakened by the constant battle with bureaucracy, just sit back a while and think of what and who you are fighting for. I guarantee that if again the reasons are true, you will soon be back on your feet, full of fuel and ready to kick any ass in your way.

Once you see your child, as ultimately you will if you don't give up, be gentle. Remember you are a sea of love and emotion ready and indeed desperate to flood them like a tidal wave.

They however are stuck in the middle of this, trying so hard to show and say the right signs and words to each parent. They will, if it has been some months or even longer be a little unsure as to what is right. Gently does it. A little at a time and it will all come back.

PIECE OF THE JIGSAW

Now November 1999, the month of my birthday and the only gift worth anything to me would be to hear the boys say "Happy birthday Dad."

I clearly would not be with them, but just to hear their voices would mean so much. But I didn't.

So I choked on the hurt for a few days and eventually decided to use this moment towards my case, in that the boys should have been encouraged to at least be allowed to send a card and call their dad on his birthday. I duly noted and filed it.

December is for all families. I suppose it's when thoughts really turn towards Christmas. For me it was always my eldest son' birthday first, right before Christmas, then Christmas could happen.

Maybe that's why even to this day, now the boys are grown and Christmas has lost its magic, I prefer a New Year party rather than a Christmas one.

Would I be able to see him or speak to him, would a birthday card even get to him? I doubt it very much but I sent one anyway of course.

Contact was becoming rarer and I was sinking again. I had taken advice and needed proof that the boys treatment was not in their best interests. I now had to be strong, patient, calm and professional, as well as the loving Dad I always dreamed I would be if and when tested.

I had been a police officer for over twelve years at this point. I had seen an awful lot of suffering, anguish, helplessness and indeed suicide brought on by exactly these circumstances I was in. These demons were not going to get me. I was going to have to step up, be counted and eventually compile the case of my career. Quiet and indeed clear thought was now to be my most potent weapon.

At the appointed time and date, not long before Christmas 1999 I stood expectant in a McDonalds car park in Berkshire. Much as I hated the thought of the boys being handed over like cargo, at least they were straight from one car to another on allotted Fridays and Sundays. I was no weekend father and totally refused to accept this as my future roll. I am a loving, caring, strong and stable father. I will be proved so.

I will get the boys and bring them up safely and in a balanced environment. I will. Unfortunately, Christmas had come along during a period of consolidation. By that I mean I was back from the ill fated trip to Scotland and true to my word I was preparing my argument for court. I used the analogy of a jig saw, that it was, but I had underestimated the size and scale of this particular puzzle. The task ahead was monumental. I was intending taking custody of our two sons from their mother.

A move seen as quite impossible by most of the legal profession, and at best difficult was the opinion of the various care agencies I spoke to. Each agency would supply me with a list of circumstances, of which one or more needed to be in existence, and the steps to which I had to go to prove it. Followed by another list of measures I needed to present as proof of my greater suitability as the 'parent with care.' Each item on these lists was to become a piece of the puzzle.

The legal people were easily taken care of. I was, without wanting to sound arrogant, perfectly confident of speaking in court and of putting my case forward. I didn't need them at this stage, maybe later, but not for now. In fact, I thought I could very much do without their meddling. Sending acidic letters which did nothing more than keep the other side at boiling point and fully on their guard. Plus I didn't relish the monthly bill at somewhere in the region of thirty pounds per letter. So, they were dispatched!

The other solicitor would now have to deal with me as I was technically un-represented. This is something they don't like. They could no longer cook up a war of words which did nothing but keep the bills high. I was determined to be as honest, forthright and parental as I possibly could when dealing with the opposing solicitor.

In fact I wanted to become a right royal pain in the arse. This way without ever appearing to the court to be unreasonable and thus damage my unblemished character, I would be able to push them to the very limit in my demands. Demands which in the absence of any 'real' court orders I was fully entitled to make, and, have granted.

Meanwhile still in McDonald's car park with the winter sun fading and a bleak chill blowing, I saw their car moving slowly around the roundabout some two hundred metres away. They took the required exit and finally into the driveway towards the car park where I stood. The boys were in the back. The car slowly pulled up in front of me, they were so close now. Close enough to reach in and engulf them in my arms, that is had the windows not been there!

The sight of both boys looking out of the back window, crying, as the car continued past me out of the car park and away will live with me forever. I stood motionless and disbelieving. The presents I had wrapped and were waiting at home, they would not get. The abundance of hugs and love I had stored in my heart, they would not get until next time, maybe. Would there be one? Why had this been done on this visit of all visits? I was in agony, foiled by an act so cruel and utterly pointless.

How on earth were the boys feeling? Why did she do this to them too?

Time stood still in my world. Whilst seemingly all around me parents and children rushed between the warmth of the restaurant and their equally warm cars. Parents taking this constant contact for granted, and children oblivious to the blanket of love which was keeping the chill from biting their young bones.

A few minutes later I started to gather my thoughts and feelings, despite the icy wind trying its best to freeze the trickle of tears to each side of my face. No feelings of hatred, they were there definitely, but thankfully for the time being buried.

I could feel deep rage. I wanted to roar, like a lion stirred reluctantly into combat. However, I had vowed to be strong but dignified. My preference to keep my own counsel was so far holding strong.

"That's fucking it" I heard myself repeat. Embarrassed, instantly hoping and praying that none of the other occupants of this car park heard my utterance. Whilst I can hold my own in any rugby club conversation and indeed sing song, I am generally not one for swearing. I really don't like it, even now when the boys who are twenty one and eighteen let slip the odd profanity I hear myself questioning the need to swear.

I knew it was futile to go after them, a public display of rage and frustration would only result in the police being called, and it have to be logged and no doubt the solicitor would hear about it before her first cup of coffee had been consumed the following Monday morning.

Although there was no such order in place to prevent me from approaching the house, I have no doubt that the boys thought there was one and would be frantic with worry if they saw me approach. Firstly, I would not put this pressure on the boys, and secondly, nor would I provide the reaction I was being sorely provoked for.

These two reasons alone were a barrier. A barrier I saw, and came up to many times but never sought to cross or break it down. A barrier which again served to protect me from allegations that I had been to their house causing problems. A painful barrier nonetheless.

This incident had driven so deep into me that my heart was sinking so fast I felt sick. I began the drive home. As I drove I began to think, to analyse and to plan. Maybe it was my way of putting the rage aside and using it positively. Or was I now becoming a hard - headed evidence gatherer instead of a loving dad?

Instinct taking over from emotion? Evidence gathering must not become a greater priority than my love for the boys and ultimate desire to gain custody, but it must be part of the plan.

The professional calm with which I was now recording these instances was becoming a concern to me. The sight of the boys crying should have been and indeed was one of the worst sights I have ever had the grave misfortune to witness, but I recalled a phrase offered to me many years ago as guidance in such stressful situations.

As a young and fairly inexperienced officer, I lost a case at court. The defendant left the courtroom smirking at me. I was beside myself with anger and frustration, and I don't mind admitting I was letting everyone back at the station know about it.

On hearing my rantings a battle-wizened old sergeant took me aside and said,

"listen yer my babs (Bristolian for listen here youngster) and remember this; softly softly catchy monkey."

Once I had calmed, he explained I should take this on the chin, learn from it and eventually if I keep professional I will be there waiting ready to capture all the evidence next time this character offends, as he surely will. Take it personally or get emotional and you will lose again.

This stood me in good stead over my career, but now I was looking at all these incidents in the same way, professionally before emotionally.

Eventually I reconciled myself that I had to be professional, but it didn't mean I loved the boys any less. Many times as a serving officer I witnessed family trauma and crying children, as well as frustrated and equally tearful adults. On these occasions the uniform acted as the barrier, added to it, professionalism, and the fact that I was not emotionally attached to these families enabled me to see an objective course based on law and social requirements, and for the most part follow the course to a satisfactory resolution.

However, on this occasion I couldn't rely on being emotionally unattached, nor was uniform a protective barrier, so I simply had to rely on professionalism. It was hurting so deep and so bad that I had to try, despite having my rawest of emotions exposed, to be the policeman.

All these incidents of the boys being denied contact with me were now moving into the public domain. Each episode was being played out in public, where I needed. This was the last thing I wanted but as we had all been brought to this stage by events outside of my control, I had to meet like with like whilst always seeking to screen the boys from as much as possible.

No longer were we using phone lines, nor a series of silent no-shows. Now each episode was to a very unappreciative audience. An audience is a group or even a single person who sees exactly what is performed. An audience could also be classed as a witness. Now I had them. Each lie to school staff would be documented. Each false claim of a court order was likewise duly noted. The boys' aunt's rapidly changing views on the level of care being given to the boys, all noted.

I had to use these displays of arrogance and petulance correctly. I knew I must never react inappropriately, nor must I ever seek to engineer a situation to use to my advantage because I would then, unforgivably, be responsible for the boys hurting.

I vowed to the boys when I realised they were not going to be allowed unconditional contact with me that no matter how much pressure was put on them, I would not pressurise them from my side. Putting them in a vice like situation would be wholly disruptive. This situation, revolving around them, was not of their making.

I accepted in the dark months after I left the family home that I had to shoulder that responsibility no matter what the outcome. There isn't a day goes by that I don't feel a degree of guilt but I left for reasons that will remain private, but I don't take all the guilt. I saw pressurising them from both sides as selfish, cruel and therefore not something I was prepared to do, no matter the provocation.

TRANQUILITY IN SOLITUDE

Christmas had fast approached. A mere three days to go and the time off work which I had organised to spend with the boys would be upon me. A time I had been so looking forward too, but sadly wasn't to be.

I was becoming increasingly enveloped in my battles. The daily letters and relentless phone calls, whether I was sleeping or not became tiresome. These callers had little or no respect for my shift pattern. Not from friends, but the Child Support Agency or my ex-wife' solicitors firm.

Letters filled with state sponsored or legally acceptable bullying. Solicitors could, and still can, weave webs of such eloquent threats. I don't think I have ever dealt with a profession so devoid of morals. I have seen them operate in the criminal world, and now the civil world too. For example, house purchase and the latest vile trend, touting for 'injury' business on daytime television. Family law specialists – a publicly acceptable way of stating a clear willingness to use every emotional blow possible to inflict damage on a loving and caring parent. Be it male or female, it is of no concern to them and I was on the receiving end.

To fall out of love is not a crime, therefore not having

committed a crime I saw no reason to be treated like a criminal, but treated like one I was. As with anyone reading this with parallels in their own life. Treatment dished out with a sole aim of rendering an otherwise loving and caring parent, a wreck. A broken man or woman, now heaving under a huge weight of self doubt who just gives in or is rendered so terrified of solicitors that eventually they just agree to any outrageous demand placed upon them.

In the criminal law world we used to call this kind of treatment of prisoners, duress, and it made convictions very unsafe. The solicitors, in my opinion, despite what they may say don't care about the reality of the real lives, broken hearts or misery. So long, of course as the fees or legal aid keeps coming in.

I appreciate it's a business world and they are indeed, sadly, a business we have in our midst and therefore must tolerate, but wouldn't it just be so refreshing if they were honest about their aims, and their methods.

"Three days to Christmas and I am just not interested." I recall her face as I said these words to Louise as she gleefully prepared to welcome her children to our home for the festive period.

She was kneeling, arranging gifts around the base of the tree. A scene so typical in millions of households. I however, simply couldn't embrace Christmas whilst aching to spend some time with my precious boys. It hurt to an intolerable degree so I had decided to take myself, my moods, my bike and the diaries I had begun to compile back to the tranquility of the Highlands.

Louise was less than impressed but like a lot of decisions I was beginning to make, I was making them with the best of intentions and single minded determination. Sadly the best of intentions part was often missed because I was becoming a demon to live with. I couldn't in any way contemplate that she would miss me. I was a hollow shell, devoid of the fun and character she would tell me were major players in my personality. I was somewhere else emotionally and mentally so I may as well be there physically too.

Stern words were exchanged, during which I don't recall her crying on the outside but knowing her as I did, her facial expression passed her feelings so clearly. She was being torn apart inside, by me. She was trying desperately to love me, but I was knocking it all back. I was becoming un-loveable. In my mind it was to prevent her being embroiled in what I believed would become a very dirty war. I was trying to protect her, and hoped that she would be safe and happy if and when I arrived back in her world.

As it was in this case, and I'm sure is the case in many struggling relationships, she didn't need protecting, but what she did need I couldn't see until too late. Had I confided in her, accepted her help and let her fight alongside me then maybe I wouldn't have hurt her so often and so deeply. I didn't realise but I was slipping headlong into a depression that was ultimately going to change me forever. Shame I was the last person to see, or accept this.

To this day I cannot recall the long journey north, other than the arrival in Newtonmore, at the hostel, my safe haven. I have faint memories of lighting a cigar whilst in a traffic jam somewhere near where the M5 and M6 motorways merge at Birmingham. I am not sure why I began to smoke these! Who knows? I was continually chasing ideas and ideals as they appeared in my personal hamster wheel.

My small Rover car could not do Bristol to Newtonmore, four hundred and fifty miles or as near as on one tank, therefore I must have stopped for fuel. I must have eaten. I must have stopped for comfort breaks. I didn't actually remember a lot.

What I do know though, is that as always I felt a deep relief turning off the main road into Newtonmore. If only for the reason that I could soon get off my ass! Ten hours driving takes its toll. I would wind down the window to allow my car and lungs to fill with fresh, ice–cold, Highland air. Suddenly aware of the depth of the darkness punctuated by a few street lamps shrouded in a hanging mist, I drove slowly along the high street.

The air was sharp, clear and with a welcoming hint of coal and wood smoke. Probably not eco-friendly but welcoming to me. I knew I was where I felt safe. No mobile phones and although Louise knew where I was, she certainly wouldn't be trying to contact me.

My car slowed to a crunchy halt on the familiar gravel car park. The security light activated and out of the darkness appeared the owners, my dear friends Kathryn, and Peter known to the rest of us as 'Ice face.' A term of affection given to Peter after a photo of him appeared on his website with his beard a mass of icicles.

They knew once again that not only was I here at Christmas, but I was alone. The motivation for my stay was not pleasant but they never asked nor judged. In the coming years I was to see a lot of them and for that I consider myself very lucky to have had them in my life.

I received my instructions that evening in the hostel kitchen, whilst downing a cup of coffee before unloading the car.

"If anyone arrives it's ten pound per night, here is a receipt pad, we will be back in a few days, you have the place to yourself."

With that sorted they were in the car and off into the same crisp air I had just been enjoying.

Was that panic ambling through me? Was my journey here to the comfort of this hostel to allow Christmas to slip by un-noticed, or was I seeking comfort with the family who had just driven away on a well-earned Christmas break.

My thoughts trailed "Do I really want this solitude?"

I paused for a moment.

"No bloody choice now, they've gone, so it's time to get unpacked and sort the bike out for tomorrow."

Once done and after a meal, a couple of beers and a dram of my favourite malt, sleep soon arrived. Too much sleep in fact, another sadly as yet unrecognised symptom of depression being the ability to sleep for huge lengths of time. Waking at noon I cursed my tardiness as I got into my brand new red and white cycling kit. The other having been cut to shreds by the paramedics several months earlier.

I was now well and truly over that crash and cycling as often as I could. Given the three inches of snow and heavy dark clouds, on went the warm cycling trousers too. Padded overshoes, breathable under vest and fluorescent jacket, topped off by a bright yellow helmet and gloves. A complete fashion statement!

Given that this was the Highlands and all the agencies were well used to dealing with snow, unlike England, the roads were clear and well gritted. So I set off for a short ride, munching a cereal bar having decided there would only be two or three hours light left and not enough time for a full breakfast. Out of the village gasping deeply as the frosty air invaded my warm and still sleepy lungs.

I gathered speed and was soon whisking towards Laggan. I appreciate that some may have an idea of where I am, others not. I was right in the heart of the British television programme 'Monarch of the Glen' country; the locality used for the classic series. Utterly inspiring scenery. Senses heightened, legs pumping and heart stabilised, I was now riding smoothly instead of gasping and holding on. This to me is such a wonderful feeling. Thirty minutes later having crossed Laggan Lochs I stood for a moment by the Monadhliath Hotel.

(Pronounced; Mon a lee ath.) I was to turn left here towards Dalwhinnie, a quiet and some say soulless little village, but more importantly the producer of my favourite malt. I crested the short sharp hill and paused a while at the entrance to the hotel drive.

A large house built in the grounds of a ruined church. A smile crackled across my frozen face as I recalled the afternoon several years ago when Dave, John and I arrived here after a long days walking over the hills in appalling weather. The owner allowed us to camp freely in the grounds near to the ruin on the proviso that we buy a meal and a few beers from the bar. Again, as in later years this seemed like a damn good deal to us.

I recalled as I sat there with boots and socks off watching my poor abused feet give off steam when a small dog lunged for one of my bright red, highly offensive socks and ran off with it in its mouth. We all roared with laughter at the thought of this now out of sight dog retching its guts up. The sock was later returned but I never saw the dog again! Yeah, good times and I dearly hope they will be back someday.

I pushed on and was soon racing towards Dalwhinnie in the languid, fading light. I had lights on the bike so not worried about the onset of darkness but I wanted to see the distillery in daylight. After a few exhilarating miles I dropped steeply into the village.

Eventually pulling up at the entrance. A fine white imposing building and maybe I do have issues but hell I could stand and look at this place all day. Brilliant white walls, a dark grey, almost blue, slate roof topped off with four or five slate turrets pointing majestically skywards. Not only out of my liking for the malt, but this building alone had a real presence. All around was barren Scots hillside covered in heather, and at over a thousand feet above sea level it is claimed to be Scotland's highest distillery.

A tour and a dram are not an option at the moment. Only because it is closed! I am sweaty, steamy and dirty from road slush and getting colder by the second. It was below freezing and destined to get even colder before night would set in. I stood astride my trusty racing bike and glanced down at the computer mounted on the handlebars. Not only was it nearly four pm, and getting dark but the lumps of white appearing on my gloves told me it was starting to snow.

Snowing up here really does mean snowing. The snow was soon heavy, getting almost Christmas card like, well it would be because it was Christmas, bless me!

The back road I had ridden on so far would have been my chosen route to return had all things been equal. However, although gritted, there was not enough traffic now to spread the grit and prevent the snow from settling. It would be gritted again prior to the morning traffic but not soon enough to help me. So, my only alternative was the A9 main trunk road.

As I looked down towards my feet I became aware of the reflection of car lights on the reflective strips sewn to the rear and side of my overshoes. My feet were now performing their own hypnotic light show. Spinning so fast, powered by my warm legs, the reflective strips would return the beams of light to passing drivers. This was exhilaration on a grand scale. For the next half hour or so I became lost in the moment.

Focused singularly on cycling in a safe and progressive manner yet at the same time powered by adrenalin and a desire to always go faster. Faster, to get to Newtonmore sooner, and faster to intensify the light show around my feet. Alas, it seemed only moments later I was freewheeling into the village, off the main road. I was relaxed yet panting, sweating and feeling the cold air settling on my face. I watched my warm breath swirl in the chilled darkness. Exercise like this is a drug, a very addictive one.

Back at the hostel having cleaned the bike of salt and dirt as well as lubricate ready for tomorrow I began to come back down to earth. Please, someone else arrive. Now and over the coming evenings I was to face the real reason for this journey. I have been pushed by circumstances to now take the initiative.

I had the peace, quiet and indeed the absolute tranquility I needed to think and to plan. I had better get on with it. No excuses, this is it. Over the following few evenings now accepting of my need to think, I began to draw my plan together. My body and mind were getting refreshed.

Fresh air, exercise and adrenalin were a heady cocktail. I needed evidence of the boy's maltreatment if I was to gain custody. More than ever now I was convinced of my ability to be a better parent. To bring them up in a forward looking and stable manner, rather than living out my own personal bitterness and attempts at revenge. I would always counsel contact with both halves of the extended family and put an end to the punishment the boys were suffering at not knowing what they could safely say and in whose company. That is no way for a child to grow up, they should have freedom to ask and to enquire about anything, as much as the freedom to run in the park, kick a ball or ride a bicycle. To get this evidence I needed, of course, witnesses.

With the space to think clearly I could see witnesses coming from various sources. Some would be official or professional witnesses such as social workers and teachers. The others would probably be family members who by seeing or hearing something would inadvertently put themselves in the frame.

Would they stand up in court?

Would they be strong for the boys?

These two questions played on my mind for quite some time. I reconciled myself that if they cared enough for the boys, not for me, they would do right by them. If they weren't prepared to speak for me, then at least they had ruled themselves out of speaking against me.

In my mind the plan began to form. I needed to get the boys heard. It was going to be an extremely complicated process to get someone independent yet professional close enough to the boys to gain their trust. Once the trust is gained, the fragile task of extracting all the information needed to present a credible case would begin.

My main reservation here was that the person who gained their trust must always have their trust and genuinely care for them and what ultimately is best for them. It simply mustn't be a case of gaining the trust, getting the facts then dropping them. That would hurt the boys and simply wasn't an option. This case ultimately, I hoped was to secure custody of my boys.

Secondly their aunt, Pam. A strong minded lady who despite her dislike of me as the separation evolved I felt would stand firm in the boy's interests. I feel I should go further in support of Pam in that I knew she would always stand up for the boys.

I would still need to prove to her that the boy's interests would be best served with me and I knew that she loved the boys deeply but was growing increasingly concerned at their current level of care and treatment. She loved them being at her home after school, at weekends and indeed any time and I had absolutely no reason to doubt her love for the boys. However, in direct conflict with her love of seeing the boys was the fact that I lived a hundred miles away and it would be my intent to bring them to me as opposed to me moving to Berkshire. I simply could not resign from my current position and start again.

I was at last thinking quietly and cohesively. Whilst I knew there were many obstacles I had yet not encountered, I was satisfied that I was beginning to deal with a very complicated obstacle; myself. Anyone in this position, and I'm sure there are many thousands, must deal with themselves first of all. As I have already mentioned you must want to get custody for all the right reasons, not just points scoring over your ex. Once you have arrived at that point then the personal side has to be opened up in a way we generally don't like, to be honest, really honest, about ourselves.

Do I have any skeletons in my cupboard? If so get them out now, dust them off and get them publicly cleansed. You may as well do it now under your own control because if and when this issue comes to the crunch in court, as many cases do, you can be assured that the other side, the adversary, will ambush you with them. Leave nothing to chance.

Similarly, don't go looking for skeletons in anyone else's cupboard which may or may not be there. Stick to only provable evidence. If it has to come from a professional, social worker, teacher etc. then let them give the facts. If they at first seem unwilling let the court know; it's amazing how persuasive a letter on behalf of a judge can be. Once you get these pieces of evidence, collate them carefully, guard them and when needed use them clinically, and without mercy. The only person or persons whose feelings you need to consider are those for whom you are fighting. Protect young souls. In later years, as they grow they will find out the truth one way or another at a speed and in a manner their increasing maturity can handle.

The final day in the Highlands saw me reach new levels of physical and mental fitness. Mental fitness was at the time paramount but I felt that physical fitness would support the mental process when the going got tough. We all have different ways of staying strong in the face of desperate provocation. This was mine.

From Newtonmore to Inverness was a harsh forty mile ride, complete in a little over two hours. I would gleefully greet each stretch of uphill riding (and if you know this section of the A9 you will know there are plenty). I would power up, accelerate over the top and race down the other side, only to arrive in a dip yet eager to repeat the process.

Arriving into Inverness was a superbly fast descent of several miles. Left towards the Great Glen, taking the B road along the eastern shore of Loch Ness, speeding along towards Spean Bridge another thirty miles were to disappear.

Fort Augustus was nothing more than an 'S' shaped chicane from the west side of the glen to the east. Navigated with nothing more than a flick of the handlebars across the Caledonian Canal, and nosing ever closer to Spean Bridge.

"When will I wander this region again?" my mind wondered.

Well here I was close to the turn of the century and even I couldn't have forecast this scenario. New Year was always so special and to be spent with the boys, but here I was, alone.

However concentration had to return to the cycling. I didn't want to come off again! Spean Bridge arrived and without a thought it was behind me as I swung left towards Laggan another twenty plus miles.

Fuelled only by water and muesli bars I destroyed the last few miles into Laggan. Again, passing the Monadhliath Hotel, a wry smile broke across my face re-routing the rivers of sweat as I recalled the dog running away with my smelly sock many years before.

Newtonmore was now a mere five miles further and it was getting dark. I was beginning to feel hungry as I cruised the last few miles in. Close to a hundred miles in the cold and wearing extra cycle clothing was a good day out in anyone's books.

I walked up the path to the hostel after carefully garaging my beloved bike. I could feel my thighs burning but they had done me proud today. All that remained was to shower, pack the car, a big feed and a couple of beers. The following day was New Years Eve. I drove home ready to fight like a man in the right. I recall thinking that if my head and heart are as strong as my thighs then the opposition had better beware.

MUTED RECEPTION

I walked in through the back door to be met with what could only be best described as, a muted reception. Evidence of Christmas was all around but Louise's children had gone to their father for New Year. The tree was still surrounded with piles of open presents left almost as comforters for her.

I recall her asking whether I had a good time, I answered and enquired likewise. Underneath this piecemeal conversation was genuine heartfelt concern for each other, shadowed in anger at the parallel situations that neither of us could understand.

I still couldn't see how she could miss me even though I believed her when she told me she did. She, unable to feel my feelings was frustrated by my inability to explain. The ability to talk openly was a gift I had yet to receive.

I know she tried desperately to understand my worsening condition for reasons known but to herself. I have no idea why she didn't leave me. She was a beautiful woman who had no trouble attracting male attention if she so wished and I no longer believed she could possibly see anything in me. She read about depression and brought me literature home. I'm not an avid reader at the best of times but with all my reading time taken up with daily correspondence with the Child Support Agency and certain solicitors, these heartfelt gestures of constructive reading were the last in a very long line and, sadly never read.

I saw how she desperately hung in there. I didn't understand at that point the way that the female generally is more readily inclined to share a problem, within a trusted circle, in the hope that help or some degree of understanding, if not a solution, could be found. 'Men are from Mars and Women from Venus.' is I grant you a somewhat tongue in cheek analysis of the differences between male and female psyche, but ignore it at your peril.

I feel tearful now, six and a half years on from this point, and three years since we split for good. I knew that someone, some circumstance, or a combination of these would ultimately destroy our relationship. Even though I had begun to love her dearly, and she was warm and loving towards me, all the feelings I craved, I never quite felt that she truly loved me as I loved her and who could blame her after all I was putting her through.

I woke sharply at midnight as my deep sleep was invaded by a truly spectacular display of fireworks lighting up the world on the outside of my bedroom window. Looking out I saw Louise and a neighbour having a good old dance, gin and tonic in hand, as the millennium slipped by. The millennium was special but I had other things to concern me; things vastly more important than a moment on a calendar.

I could hear Louise's laugh above all others. Not that it is loud or particularly noticeable, just very special to me. I looked for a few moments watching them dance through the snow and out of sight towards the rear of the house. I wished I could make her that happy. I loved her so dearly and so deeply. When all this was over maybe we will be left alone to live and love in peace. I knew how hard she was trying to love me, but I also knew that my preoccupation with fighting to secure the boys custody was making it so difficult for her. I did love her, sadly more than I could have possibly shown her at that time.

My task however was the safety and security of my boys and I defy any parent worth their salt to behave differently given the same circumstances.

~

Cycling through the crisp new millennium air on the way to work early next morning I wondered, as many of us do every year, what will the next twelve months hold for me? I sort of had an idea it would not involve too much more than court rooms, solicitors, the Child Support Agency and countless letters on headed paper. I didn't have to wait long. The first was not from a solicitor or any of the usual suspects, but from the boy's aunt, Pam.

Bracknell Forest social services had been in touch with her to get my address. This letter was a request for me to call them or give my permission for them to have my address. I could feel the fear from the paper.

I called her; she was trembling as she relayed a story given to her by a local hairdresser. I knew witnesses would come from surprising quarters. The story involved the youngest of my boys being hit so hard that the assailants hand was left stinging. Quite a boast! Whoever that hairdresser was, and I still to this day do not know who it is, I am grateful from the bottom of my heart for showing the courage needed to promote the boys safety. That hairdresser was quite rightly horrified on hearing this boastful account that she contacted social services.

At last, heartbreaking that it was, this was the breakthrough I needed. I called social services but sadly it was some days before I got to speak to the social worker concerned.

An agonising wait as I tortured myself with conjecture and painful 'what if' scenarios. A wait which, when I finally spoke to and later met the appointed social worker, Karen, was well worthwhile. At that time I felt reluctant to fully commit to and trust the social services.

However as I got to know Karen I quickly became aware I had a strong minded ally in her. Whilst she was robust in her protection aims for the boys and condemnation of their treatment on occasions, she was also quick to challenge me if I became too sure of myself and dismissive of the challenge ahead. I was continually reminded of my own words that this must not be a battle between my wife and myself with the boys being the prize to the victor.

It was a tragic set of circumstances with the boys the central figures and all efforts must be applied rigorously and solely for their well-being. The fact that either my wife or I would ultimately be devastated was of much lesser consequence. We were both equally under scrutiny now. Karen was now another witness, and indeed a formidable one.

Initially I felt angered at the level of scrutiny I seemed to be under, but as I watched Karen work, and the process was painfully slow in my opinion, I started to feel safer and so began to open up to her in a way I had not thought possible. Here I was, a street hardened police officer of many years, having witnessed suffering and much publicised inactivity by social services, slowly opening my head, heart and soul to this lady.

I eventually trusted her with the most fragile of my emotions. I simply had to trust her and what was more surprising was that I really wanted to. She was strong, which I needed, as did the boys. We needed her to stand firm in the face of venomous objection from some quarters, which was sure to come as her enquiries progressed. She had the most caring of smiles which is a strange thing for me to recall but whenever we met I ended up in tears of emotion going through the latest episodes of her attempts to get close to the boys.

Every session would end without fail, with her slowly breaking into a reassuringly warm smile. I knew she cared.

Early spring of 2000, after the now very familiar drive up the motorway, I was embarking on a very unfamiliar route this particular day. As the result of care agency work and investigations it had been decided that a case conference had to be convened to discuss the care and future of the boys. Plan wise, this was exactly what I needed to happen, getting the issues into a more public arena. Privately I was raging that what the agencies had so far seen had brought them to this stage in only a couple of months. I was also terrified for the boys. I hated the thought that there was suspicion that they weren't being cared for sufficiently.

The short time from receiving the letter informing me of the decision and date had seemed like an age, but now time seemed to be running out of control. It was an element of control that I needed to feel I had. I needed to feel I was driving the care issues but now I feared that it would be taken out of my hands.

Once inside the building which was modern, clean and for the most, staffed by warm smiles, I felt conscious that I was being observed by all as someone called here to answer to some sin or other mis-demeanor. I kept telling myself that I was the good guy trying to look after my children. I was shown to a small waiting room, by a polite and softly spoken lady who offered me a cold drink, but as they didn't seem to have malt whiskey on the menu I declined. I assumed I was being kept out of the way to avoid unsightly clashes with my ex-wife, assuming again that she would be in attendance too.

I dearly hoped she would be as I think an adjournment at this early stage wouldn't have filled me with confidence regarding the influence of these agencies.

It was bizarre but as I sat waiting, nervously trying to make last minute notes, my pen was slowly being rendered uncontrollable by the degree of sweat coming from my palm. My anxiety level had clearly risen to an unhygienic level and my choice of a mid blue cotton shirt was clearly a mistake, demonstrated by every move of my arms. Although not a particularly nice thought or vision, it showed how important this was to me for the sake of all our futures.

Why on earth was vanity bothering me now? Was I worried that the sight of my armpits would be a sign of weakness, would that go against me? No, not at all, indeed quite the opposite, I hoped it would show I cared so much.

"Ok Mr Reed you can come in now." These words echoed and I shook as I stood up.

I had been lost in a world of self-examination, and totally failing to notice that our intended meeting room, just across the corridor was slowly filling. These words softly spoken and wrapped in the familiar warm smile erupted into my silent world. It was Karen. She had assured me she would be there but until this point I hadn't seen her. I was relieved to see her, but terrified that this was now the start of an unknown process.

She calmly showed me to my seat which I cautiously pulled back, sat down and arranged my books, pens etc. very carefully. I was concerned that with hands of oil I would send everything scattering across the large table. Karen sat opposite me, now stone faced and efficient, this was business mode. There were strangers, several of them and two familiar faces, my wife and her aunt, Pam.

Her aunt; why? She had seen so much maltreatment; she

had been there when I arrived to collect the boys for the holiday that never was. She had seen so much. She had related the hairdresser scenario to me and the social services. Why on earth was she sat next to my wife?

I needed her on my side, to speak in support of the boys or at the very least not to have turned against the welfare of the boys. I had been utterly convinced that even though she may have issues with me, she was totally focused on the well-being of the boys. So how could she contemplate speaking in support of my wife, if that was indeed the reason for her presence here today? I was severely rattled by this, and hadn't a clue what was to come. I sat and worried silently.

As was to become customary at these meetings we in turn gave a short introduction including our name, our role and relevance to the meeting. I did particularly well I think, I managed to get out "Geoff Reed – Dad."

After I had spoken those first few shaky words, I thought that as my first and last opportunity to make a first impression on these people who are absolutely vital to the boys future and safety, I had made a right balls' of it. So now they are all thinking; "That is the Dad" – sweats like a shower and incapable of speaking, good start!

I didn't know who the others were. I hadn't heard a thing other than Pam saying "Support for Mum."

Jesus Christ, support?

How the hell am I going to get her support for the boys!

More worryingly was the thought that if she, who had

been the one to show real guts in calling in the social services in the first place, was to change her position then everything she said to get us this far may as well be ignored. I sat there for thirty to forty minutes struggling to take in what was being said.

They discussed so much more than I knew of, so much more than I thought possible. I was in total disbelief. As I have stated this book is not about blame. Furthermore, this book is not about and will never be about the private individual incidents. It is however wholly about my emotions as I began the perilous journey of a father attempting to wrest custody of two young boys, my sons.

Any person from a family experiencing similar matters will, I have no doubt, have different individual incidents. To try to examine them in such a public manner would in my mind be perversely voyeuristic, as well as getting dangerously close to apportioning blame, for which there should be no room in children's proceedings.

I simply couldn't keep my composure any longer, as finally the chair of the meeting decided that both boys be placed on the child protection register. I sank my head. As my head lowered I caught a glance of my wife. She sat stone faced and seemingly emotionless.

I rested my forehead on my forearms. All I could see was a dark place made darker by my dark blue sleeves which were getting darker by the second with each tear.

The room emptied accompanied only by the noise of

chairs and feet shuffling, but not much conversation. This was not a meeting to be proud to be at, nor one to take any form of satisfaction from at the conclusion. I began to let my tears flow. I didn't want to hold them back.

Safe in the knowledge that my grief was now private as I heard the door close I cried uncontrollably. I thought the room was empty. Then a soft word and a gentle hand on my shoulder. It was Karen, she placed a box of tissues in front of me. I hadn't even notice her come back into the room. I cried, sobbed and dribbled into countless tissues as she explained to me that this was the first step and a very positive one.

These words from Karen were proof that emotion is the sworn enemy of reason. Just as I, as a police officer had managed to stay focused through other people's problems, now she was doing what I needed most but had plainly missed. I simply couldn't see through my tangled web of raw emotion until she sat me down and quietly explained. This is something I have to thank all the care professionals for, as at every stage they would be acutely aware of the people involved being completely knotted and confused.

If you are in this position, please make sure that you listen to them and whilst possibly not fully agreeing, at least understand the process that has to be followed and why. Understand is a hugely important word here; make sure you ask questions, and keep asking until you do. Once you understand that, then you are able to keep the pressure on in the right places. You will have little enough energy as it is, make sure you don't waste it by pushing, well meaning but in the wrong direction.

So, I eventually grasped that all agencies were now involved, providing the legal basis for more powers to monitor and therefore more opportunities to gather the much needed evidence, if it was there, and gathered in such a way that the boys felt as little stress as possible.

Then with the evidence having been collected in a safe and proper manner it will be accepted in future proceedings.

It was at times such as these, and there were many brought on by meetings, letters or even just phone calls when I felt so weary with it all that, had I not truly had the boy's best interests at heart I would possibly have cracked. No points scoring over an ex-partner would ever be worth this fatigue, I doubt it would even survive. Love however, is a potent fuel and therefore a source of endless energy. I still wasn't getting to see the boys very often.

Why couldn't they do something I repeatedly asked myself? The other thing you will need is trust. Let the professionals do their job and you just have to adopt a support role for want of better words, but one quietly driving it forward.

I drove in silence back to Bristol, a six foot, sixteen stone wreck. If this was a positive step forward, then I just cannot wait for a real negative kick in the balls. Even though I now understood what was happening I still ached for contact with my sons. That thought would never change.

TAKE HELP WHEN NEEDED

At least now I knew, as I drove each time up the motorway, what was to happen in the meeting or at least had a reasonable idea. I even became quite good at speaking to all the folk sat around the table. I developed the ability to be positive, questioning and even forceful without being aggressive.

However dull the process, my real fear came from the continuing revelations. Each seemed more difficult to take, not always more serious but always more painful and always accompanied by the frustration of being just a dad who simply did not have the power within him to halt this awful series of events. To halt the physical and mental torment being suffered by the boys.

To a much lesser degree was also the suffering of those on the outside. People who genuinely cared but were again excluded from the caring process by the legal process. A legal system which boasts protection of the children but openly excludes the people who really care.

During the ensuing months of painfully slow progress I became even more single minded in my pursuit of the boys. Every morning as the first flickers of light pierced my eyes until sleep finally bade farewell to the day I was wholly consumed by, and focused on my battle for the boys. Despite my best efforts it was now really beginning to affect me at home, at work and in my relationship with Louise. My dear Louise who's very smile could make everything ok, just for one blissful moment at a time; whose warmth and love I was beginning to ignore albeit unintentionally. I was fighting this alone and to the exclusion of everyone around me, even her. The cracks were beginning to appear but I couldn't see them. I just wanted to live alone so that no one else could be hurt by this agonising process and the accusations being fired at me or us.

To my mind this was a genuine effort to help others by removing them from the firing line. Louise knew I was going under.

"Ok then, you go to the doctor, get sorted out and if then you still want me to go, I will."

Words she said to me one morning as we sat discussing my desire to live alone and therefore protect everyone. It was a very brave and heartfelt gesture, but one that seemed like it was make or break.

I could clearly see that she was hurting so deep but I genuinely thought I was handling it well by offering her a safe way out. Symptomatic of a depressed person's rationale, I can now see. Either way I realised it was her way of telling me she was at the end of her ability to cope with my distant behaviour. I don't, and never did think that it was the end of her desire to help me, just the end of her ability to. She was exhausted, and another casualty in all this.

I was never one for going to the doctors. I always seemed to come out feeling worse than when I went in. The thought of being propped up by medication was appalling to me. Two paracetamol tablets are enough to make me sleep the clock round, so anything stronger doesn't bear thinking about. It took me several weeks and clashes with Louise before I eventually went to the doctor.

Once in the doctor's consulting room I think it was probably the easiest diagnosis he will have made in a long time. Looking back on it now I was displaying all the signs and symptoms of depression. I was very tearful, insular, extreme fatigue, irrational thoughts and reasoning. Not quite paranoia but protection was so high on my list, for everyone, that it was becoming a real concern.

After a very short time he gave his diagnosis, 'Reactive Depression.' These words echoed from his mouth. I can still see his lips moving as he spoke them. I was in shock, all around me went blurred, into a kind of soft focus. I couldn't believe it. I was so fit, so strong and had made light of everything that the Scottish Highlands could throw at me. I was completely ready for this battle or so I thought. I was so worried that I was about to be undone by a weakness I couldn't control.

I couldn't show a weakness now. I hadn't taken a day off sick from work despite all the pressure. My work I loved and it was indeed an escape on a daily basis. I didn't want, nor could I show a weakness for anyone to exploit. A medical condition, especially a depressive one was the last thing I needed, well almost. I sort of thought a criminal record might be pretty bad too!

I could just see all the agencies taking a different look at my suitability as a stable parent and adversaries rubbing their hands in gleeful anticipation of a speedy conclusion to these proceedings. If the level of care the boys were now getting was such that inclusion on the child protection register, hereafter just referred to as 'the register' was deemed appropriate then, if I was to be suddenly taken out of the equation by medical or mental failings then what left for the boys? Care home? My patient and carefully constructed plan was being thrown to the wind, and my mind was spinning out of control with worry.

After a few moments discussion, reassuring discussion, I was prescribed a new tablet on the market for depression - I hate even using the phrase anti-depressants. It wasn't addictive, had little or no side effects and I wouldn't need to give up the emergency response side of my profession. These last few words were indeed crumbs of comfort being offered as the doctor wrote on the small green pad. Why do we always try so hard to decipher doctor's handwriting?

I left the surgery with a cocktail of relief, emotion and above all worry coursing through me. I was convinced more than ever that everyone was looking at me, as the new loser on the block. All I had were questions as to what the future may hold. Sadly I didn't as yet have any answers.

Thirty minutes later though, I had the short term answer

97

before me in the shape of a box containing whatever he had prescribed. The previously ineligible scroll was now in huge clear letters emblazoned across a cigarette sized box for all to see, even the nosy cow looking over my shoulder in the chemist trying to glean from the glossy packaging some clue to my ailment.

Clutching this box in my fast shrinking hand I leered at her and snapped,

"Sorry to disappoint you" as I whisked off out of the chemist.

I suppose it is my own fault for opening the paper bag before I got home. Maybe I was more curious than she was! Still, if it kept her in gossip for a few days then no harm done.

It is true that until you begin to take the remedy you are sometimes wholly unaware of just how poorly you are becoming. Once at home I sat reading the information slip provided inside each of the boxes of tablets desperately seeking a reason not to take them. There were the usual array of precautions, machinery, driving and alcohol etc. One, however was to stand out above all the rest: sleepiness for the first few days of taking them, until the body gets used to the dosage, which as it goes was one a day.

That is no problem as I was to take one before bed, whether it be night or morning depending on my shift.

One of the rare moments of laughter between Louise and me, because sadly there weren't many by this stage, was the speed in which I was asleep having taken my nightly tablet. My personal light was often out before the bedroom light.

Eventually the tablets did begin to do their job. I suddenly felt I had reserves of strength, in actual fact I was only back to normal. I had been running on empty. The down side of this was that with even more strength for the fight, and beginning to take more and more of the initiative instead of waiting for a blow to respond to, my beloved Louise was fading even further into the background. A cruel twist indeed as she was the one who had guided me to the doctor.

Over the summer of 2000, I grew stronger with the help of these 'mad tabs' as my colleagues and I renamed them! I accept that this phrase for what are in effect serious medical drugs will not be to everyone's liking. If it offends you I am genuinely sorry, but it was my way of coping, and we all cope slightly differently.

Following many social services meetings and after taking lots of advice I decided that I would have much better chance of custody of the boys if I wasn't a shift worker. Although we lived as partners, Louise and I weren't married which was seen as a less permanent relationship by our court system.

I live in hope that as time goes by the courts will begin to see past what is purely a piece of paper and the absence of one in no way dilutes the commitment between two people in a loving and stable relationship. So here was a huge question; should we separate? I had no family in the south west area to assist me with child care but was becoming fiercely independent and even taking steps to present to the court, childcare arrangements with me robustly at the helm with just a few periods of help from childminders, and Louise.

My youngest son had ADHD and as such required a more specialised level of care, which I desperately wanted to be providing. Moving to Berkshire was a financial and professional non-starter. I had to stay put, indeed I wanted to stay here. I had a comfortable three bedroom home which was more than sufficient.

During the late summer we moved from the rented house to one six doors away and in much nicer condition. The reason being that the landlord wanted us out so the place could be renovated and then he could rent for more money. So Louise having seen this house and made estate agent enquiries we made an offer to buy, which was accepted. Who ever said that house purchase was one of the most stressful events in life?

I have to say at this point the stress levels went through the roof and I must question my ability to have coped and indeed carry on the fight without the medication. I will always be eternally grateful to Louise for insisting I went to the doctor, and for the internet being in its infancy and therefore not able to provide sufficient information to scare me out of taking the tablets.

The house purchase almost went unnoticed, except at the bank.

So where was I? We had the house, the all-important material status symbol. Not that it is necessary, a loving home is the key, but it was just my way of presenting stability to the court and indeed the care agencies. I was in a reasonably well paid profession and once the Child Support Agency was no longer a thorn in my side I would be even better off.

Yes the good old Child Support Agency, as I mentioned earlier, I saw this organisation as an animal that couldn't be fought let alone beaten, so I decided as I genuinely wanted to take responsibility for my sons, not to miss a single payment and in doing so get them on my side. And so, I gained a very powerful ally indeed. I danced to every beat of their tune, not without an occasional argument, and kept them very close to me.

A clean payment history was another reliable testimony to my suitability and willingness to prioritise. When the thorny issue of financial support for the boys, whilst I was still fighting for custody, came to the surface along the way they became a very powerful witness. It is truly amazing, and at the same time appalling the stunts the system allows to be pulled to discredit you, so you will do well to keep an open mind when you feel under attack, difficult as it will seem, and just allow yourself to think;

"Can this person or agency, be of any use later?"

To my mind I could show I had the means to provide a safe and loving home for the boys. Amenities for them were plentiful in the area. All I now needed was a Monday to Friday day job within the police service to give me the stability to offer the boys a full time dad; but how could I get that sort of job. I just couldn't see me sitting in an office all day.

ME, A TEACHER!

In the early weeks of 2001, whilst on a training course at Police Headquarters it was suggested by a guy whom I will be eternally grateful to, that I apply to be a trainer within the police headquarters' set up.

It would primarily be Monday to Friday 8am to 5pm with just the occasional weekend or unsociable hours shift.

This would suit me perfectly. Lots of female officers I knew worked similar hours to accommodate their domestic circumstances and although I didn't personally know any male single parents, there must be some, and with the current thinking of diversity I saw no reason why I wouldn't be afforded the same opportunities.

After a couple of discreet phone calls to folks in the know, I decided to apply for the post. I duly filled in the application form and within a week or two I attended, with others, the selection day. This consisted of giving a short presentation on a very dull topic as I recall, then five minutes to verbalise my thoughts on resolving several scenarios. Nothing gets sorted in five minutes in practical terms but it's the thought process they were looking for. It was then followed by an interview.

A few days later the letter arrived to say that I had failed.

That wasn't in my plan! I took the offer of a feedback interview to see where I had gone wrong as well as to ask whether it was worth applying again. This interview, and therefore the decision to ask these questions turned out to be a very important step in my journey.

It was clear that I had failed on a couple of small issues, in fact not that I had really failed, just others on the selection had been better prepared for the scenarios. It was a wholly new method to me. It was suggested that I hang in there and wait for another advert for these jobs maybe within a year or so. The 'year or so' bit immediately alarmed me as I didn't have that amount of time.

Maybe the search for a day time job may have to intensify I thought. This was a really difficult time because I loved what I did as an operational officer. Professionally I would baulk at the thought of an office job, but that had to be put aside now, my boys were my goal.

I was tipped off about an advert in the police review magazine for potential trainers to staff the regional police training colleges. If successful the post could be at any of the six or seven national training centres across Britain.

One of the centres was at Cwmbran in Gwent and my intention, was to work at this college and therefore commute daily. I only live fifteen minutes from the English side of the Severn Bridge, therefore making the whole journey about thirty minutes.

The application form could only be described as a

monster, all fifteen pages of it. I had never seen an application like it before. I had never really evidenced my suitability for any role professionally. I was a police officer and did what police officers do!

The irony also struck me that never before had I needed to evidence my suitability as a father, yet I was doing that at the very same time.

I read through the letters and requirements accompanying the application form, and quickly realised that this was a massive step professionally. It was a national job with huge responsibilities, not least of which was the wellbeing and guidance of new recruit officers from forces all over the UK in the very early stage of their respective careers within the police service. Again an ironic parallel with my intentions domestically.

I sat and thought very carefully and deeply as to whether I may be taking on too much in the way of responsibility at a time when I was still on medication for depression, albeit I felt very much stronger and was already seeking advice from the doctor about the best way to get myself off the tablets.

I was also acutely aware of how the social and legal agencies may view my new role. Would they take the view that it would be too much at such a delicate time and possibly detract from the level of care I could provide for the boys?

After much thought and several long phone calls, primarily to our social worker Karen, I decided, (and it was important that it really was my decision) that working a set pattern of regular days with no night shifts and very little weekend work, I would in fact be able to provide very well for the boys. This would then leave the opposition legal team even less to object to.

With that in mind I acted on the feedback from my earlier failed application and sought guidance on how to best fill in the application form. This process took several days, possibly even a week or two. It was exhaustive and indeed the cause of some crossed words between Louise and I.

If I wasn't working or sleeping, I would be at the computer agonising over each word and piece of evidence. Eventually it was complete and duly posted in time to meet the deadline. I think I vowed never to fill in one of those again!

Within a couple of weeks I found myself at the assessment day, at the police college in Cwmbran, Gwent, the same college I was hoping to work at. It was an un-inspiring building surrounded by an eight foot fence topped with barbed wire. The day involved another presentation, this time on a subject given to all candidates, a couple of written exercises and a torturous interview.

After the day's mauling I sat drained amongst the other dozen or so hopefuls, only to be finally told we would be informed by post in a few days!

I returned across the Severn Bridge very nervous, having placed so much importance on this job, my future felt as though it was in their hands.

Three or four days later having finished a set of night

shifts I finally stumbled into life about three on the Friday afternoon. Sadly, I wasn't to see the boys this weekend but I could reconcile myself that I was working on my master plan.

Louise had just arrived home from work, standing in the kitchen sipping my way through my first mug of coffee she suggested that we go out for tea. Nothing special in the way of food but very special in that I would be able to spend time with her in as relaxed a state of mind as possible.

When I look back on the efforts she made to help me release and enjoy myself now and again I realised she was a pure angel to me in my difficult years.

Ready to go out, you know the drill folks, keys, money, keys again, wallet etc. My mobile phone rang,

"Geoff. Hi it's Larry, Chief Inspector from the training department, just a quick call. If you were to have passed the assessment day and be offered the job could you be in Harrogate, North Yorkshire on Monday morning?"

"Yes… ere, yes. Have I, Will I?" I still wasn't fully awake. I tried desperately to glean more from him, if only clarification.

"Got to go; letter in the post, you will be contacted over the weekend."

I put the phone down and started crying, in pure relief. My plan, assuming I had understood Larry, had advanced one huge step in the pace of a two minute call.

Louise knew exactly what had been said, and the implications for us as a family unit. She gave me a hug, but something was missing. I don't know what, but there was definitely something missing from this hug. Maybe the realisation that I would be working away or that I was a giant leap closer to becoming a full time single dad, it was suddenly and very clearly on her mind. Was this call the death knell for our relationship? I loved her.

The police service, which I was so proud to be a part of, was now to take on a much more important role in my life in that it was to further contribute to my care of the boys and thus positively affect their lives too. I informed the relevant care agencies that after a ten week training period I would finally be in a day job. I sensed approval and relief from these agencies which in turn clarified in my own mind that I had made the right decision.

The following morning and sporting a good quality hangover, I opened a letter. This time, for a change with eagerness!

It went on to read; 'after due consultation, the Home Secretary is pleased to offer you a position within National Police Training.' The rest of the letter was vaguely irrelevant apart from the final sentence. 'This position has a three to five year tenure which will begin on completion of the requisite trainer's course. This course will begin at 9am Monday,' less than forty eight hours away!

A huge hurdle was now behind me and I just needed to get this long and historically difficult course behind me as well.

I got word to the boys, and having already told the various agencies, I informed solicitors. I didn't however discuss it with

Louise. Looking back on it I almost presented her with a done deal.

I was to leave the following morning to begin my training. Late on Sunday morning and after a whirlwind twenty fours of packing and phone calls, I left on the next phase of my plan. I needed and was determined to secure the boy's safety and welfare, yet the lady I loved so deep and so dear was to fade even further. After several hours driving I eventually arrived in the beautiful town of Harrogate, North Yorkshire.

Having been on these tablets for long enough in my opinion, and the depression virtually gone it was time to get rid of them. I decided that as I had seven weeks on the course followed by three weeks of post course teaching practice this was a real opportunity to rid myself of my dependency on them. There were two reasons for wanting to get rid.

The first that I simply do not like and have never liked taking medication, maybe this stems from my childhood; growing up in the green and pleasant North West Derbyshire countryside. Fishing, cycling, football, rugby and weekends camping amongst the sprawling Peak District hillside – with hay fever! A truly cruel affliction to bestow upon any child yet alone this emerging adolescent. Spring to me as a child was tablets, sprays and injections in some really sore places. All of which failed spectacularly. I was an outdoor boy and was not prepared to compromise. Sadly, spring for me as an adolescent was a journey on a river of tears and snot. Girlfriends were a non-starter, I had pockets full of handkerchiefs and eyes like dogs balls. Not a look to cultivate. Not even for a sympathy vote. As soon as I had the choice I simply didn't take them.

A second and more serious reason for needing to be rid of these tablets was the stigma attached to them and the condition they treat. Reactive depression was my diagnosed condition; however I knew I was preparing for a fight in the courts against a legal team who would no doubt use every trick in the book, fair or foul to prevent me succeeding in my bid for custody of the boys.

As I continued my preparation, and the care agencies finalised their reports I was advised to get a solicitor who would if nothing else keep me abreast of the current legal thinking in these circumstances. I knew that the legal adversaries would waste no time in highlighting it, if I were still on the tablets.

The fact that I still had an emotional illness would become a major part of their case to prove I was not sufficiently stable to care for two children who had already gone through a great deal. It would be handing over the case without a fight. I cannot recall ever walking away from a challenge in my life so far, and damn well didn't intend to start now.

I also knew that through my many discussions with social workers etc., that it would have been extremely foolish to stop taking medication if it was still needed. Whichever way was to be chosen had to be for the correct reason at the correct time, and not just for appearances.

Removing myself from medication that I genuinely

needed would be seen as irrational, irresponsible and certain not to be missed by anyone seeking to undermine me.

Harrogate, minus the tablets, I called to speak to Louise about my medication and agreed not to take the tablets anymore and more importantly she agreed not to send them to me.

I just binned them.

I cannot underestimate the suffering Louise went through as she rode the wake of my turbulence as I had tried to wean off them a few months earlier. Reduced to half a tablet per day, then every other day etc., all the normal weaning-off methods, but they never really worked.

Instead I had almost polar mood swings. I never offered any violence towards her but I know I said things that really upset her; and me when I realised what I'd said.

Despite this she was always there with a hug or a smile but I knew deep within my core as I left for Harrogate she was becoming tired, very tired of my moods. She was having to draw deeper on her own hidden reserves just to find those hugs and smiles, which in turn was eating away at her.

I honestly do not know what I would have done without her during those previous two years. I knew deep down that she was pleased I was going away and the tablets would be no more when I returned. I'm not sure how I knew, I just sensed her relief. I felt so much for her, I had so much love for her that I feel close to tears even now as I recall those bitter-sweet days.

Depression is a truly cruel illness, with always more than one victim. It was like one day being a giggling teenager getting drunk on cheap cocktails and the next I would drive off alone in reaction to the latest acidic letter from the Child Support Agency or a solicitor. Sometimes I would be away for days and she would be clueless as to my whereabouts or wellbeing.

Settling in at the four star hotel in Harrogate, The Cedar Court which was to be my home for the next seven weeks. I slowly began to realise I was moving into a different world, professionally as well as personally. This was a world of Home Office facilities, demand, supply and expense accounts. A mixture of police officers of all ranks yet always first name terms. Of civil servants too, a species I had not so far encountered. Remember; three days prior to my arrival in Harrogate I had been on nights, sorting out drunken fights and domestic strife. At least I was qualified for the latter! Whilst unpacking I reached my first dilemma do I wear uniform or not? It wasn't clear from the joining instructions. I had to make a decision and I tend to look like a bag of shit in civilian clothes, and feel comfortable in uniform, so be it, uniform it is.

If I turn up tomorrow as being the only one in uniform maybe I will rethink this, until then however I was happy with my decision. I didn't know who else would be on the course, and in a crowded hotel it is difficult to see who's who as potential class-mates.

LIFE'S ABOUT TO CHANGE

After three trips to the car park all my stuff now in my room. When I say room I mean a cavernous end room which as the course progressed and I gelled with three or four like-minded souls my room became known as the east wing wine club. So here in this room I had all the things that spelled out my life:

My uniform, on hangers neat and pressed. I knew no other way!

My bulging briefcase, stuffed not with work, but countless letters from the Child Support Agency, courts and solicitors. Papers I needed to carry on my fight even whilst away from home.

My bike, my precious racing cycle. My only way of escaping the mental pressure was to ride like the wind every day after work. Stay fit and help sleep.

A small frame on the bedside table always smiling at me was Louise. It was instinct that whenever and wherever my travels took me this small photo frame containing a smiling lady was always the last thing to be packed so the first thing to be unpacked. She was always with me, from this four star hotel to cramped climbers hostels in the Scottish Highlands and even my little back packing tent on many a mountainside. I wondered which, if any of these four things would survive the months and years ahead?

Finally, and closest to my heart was a small but precious photo of the boys, stood on their aunt's doorstep. This was in my wallet and went everywhere with me. It was getting a little creased because I would regularly remove it, look at it and think to myself, 'One day guys, one day.'

The course started, continued, and ultimately would finish, then soon it would be time to go home. There were moments on the course which were truly enlightening, as were there times that I would easily forget. I committed myself to the course because failure simply wasn't an option and think I genuinely got plenty from it, but ultimately it was a means to an end, part of my bigger plan for the future.

I arrived home to a new life, but only truly home at the weekends. The reality of my new job was made clear to me on a visit from my force training officer who told me that I would not be working in Cwmbran, as I had intended. I would be working in Oxfordshire.

This threatened initially to de-rail my plan. I had now to inform my new employers, the Home Office, that I intended to be a single parent potentially with two dependant children and so would require a suitable flat or house connected to wherever I worked. It would have been very easy to cut and run, straight back to my home force and start again. But in an organisation such as the Home Office, equality of opportunity was a big issue.

As I was working for the home office on secondment from my home force, whilst being very careful not to appear arrogant and end up with nothing, I decided to try by the correct means and procedures to make this organisation work for me, for us. The facilities were there and I would have been a fool not to make use of them. Extra money, free housing and of course expenses.

I did not relish being away from Louise Monday to Friday but the main focus in my life as always, was the boys, and if moving them to Oxfordshire was the only option to me then it would do fine. I know that earlier I had decided that to uproot professionally would be a huge mistake, but these circumstances were much different. I was moving within the service, and Home Office secondment does sound good in court!

During my training I went on a journey, a seven week journey of intense emotion. Finding out and discovering even more about myself. Challenging others as well as being challenged, was a process I never thought could be so rewarding.

From outbursts involving me bouncing a chair across the classroom to moments of silent reflection and realisation.

The realisation was that I was now mixing with some very clever people who as part of the course were 'pushing my buttons' to get at the very deepest of my values and emotions, which were pretty raw in that moment. This in turn was showing me how to get the same out of others, in the future.

Part of my future role would require me to prompt others to open up fully, not to change themselves necessarily but always to discover what was in there. Those parts of us that hide deep within under lock and key.

Seven weeks of working during the day, then cycling through the spring evenings and enjoying the tranquility of the English countryside. I would cycle the day's emotions away.

Seven weeks without a tablet!

Seven weeks without contacting Louise. Where had I been? Where had the time gone?

I no longer needed the tablets, my chemical crutches. I hoped this was permanent. In fairness I hadn't had much crap from the forces of darkness whilst on the course. Even they seemed to leave me alone.

I desperately hoped that when the course was over and the battle was to resume I would no longer need the tablets. This was a big issue for me at this stage.

I was informed that I would be working at the training centre at Heythrop Park, Oxfordshire. A beautiful, sprawling country manor of which the home office rented a wing as a police training centre. It was close to Chipping Norton, a sizeable town with all the amenities I would need. I had been to see it and noticed that all the staff lived in various cottages in the grounds. Idyllic.

Seven weeks without contacting Louise; that alarmed me. Every morning I would say "Good morning" to her picture and every evening say "Goodnight." Some may say I was soft to treat a photo in a frame with such love but I am strong enough to admit it.

However was I becoming too weak to contact the real person?

Was I afraid?

Was it guilt?

Here I was feeling pleased that I'd kicked the tablets, kept the forces of darkness at bay and provided I didn't completely self-destruct, I would pass the course.

In achieving all this I had no head space for the lady who was every day my first and last heartbeat. I simply had to speak to her before getting home. I couldn't just turn up. I was thinking about her right in that moment and my heart physically ached.

In the final week of my course, mid May 2001, following my daily routine I was out cycling in the evening sunshine, but not completely at peace within the countryside. I could bear it no longer, I was thinking about Louise constantly and having nearly died once whilst cycling with things on my mind, I didn't fancy a rerun of that incident.

I stopped in a pub car park and with sweat dripping onto my mobile phone I called home. Why was I so nervous? It was my home.

"Hello" in her normal bright cheery manner. I was reduced to tears in seconds.

"I've done it, I've passed," I was babbling excitedly whilst simultaneously apologising for seven weeks of no contact.

Her delight at my kicking the tablets seemed muted at best, "Would you like to come here on Saturday for a meal?" She asked.

This caring and kind offer, which I eagerly accepted, was in fact a huge indication of our relationship. I had become such a stranger in my own home that I was being invited there for a dinner.

I was pleased, relieved but also terrified that Louise had seen my seven week exile as a statement that I no longer wished our relationship to continue. I loved her so much but, in doing what I thought was right I may have finally ruined it all.

I have now realised that when all-consumed with a course of behaviour that in my own mind was one hundred percent correct and for the right reasons, it is not necessarily correct for others in the same equation. I am convinced, some may say arrogantly that I knew what was best for my children and that I was best placed to provide that. I also knew that this custody battle was going to last for ages. I had been given a seven week reprieve but the momentum was soon to gather again.

I had also decided that even though I was looking at possibly a year, as the legal profession doesn't work quickly, I was going to push it forward as much as I could. After all, the more the solicitors spin it out the more they get paid.

Finally the end of the week arrived and, with the certificate tucked into the bulging briefcase I left Harrogate bound for sunny Oxfordshire. Heythrop Park was bathed in late spring sunshine as I drove up to the gravel car park adjoining the 'police' wing. I struggled to contain my excitement and feelings of invincibility as driving through the grounds of the main house I spotted several cottages in the grounds and wondered which of these would eventually be home for me and my boys.

I couldn't wait to tell them, but at this point I didn't want more confusion in their lives until I had taken the necessary steps. I knew when the time was right I would take my time and gradually inform them of my intentions.

I was so excited at my new career, and my new domestic plans. I was wholly driven by my knowledge that I was best for the boys.

It was Friday afternoon as I settled into a small but homely cottage surrounded by trees, flowers and various herb bushes. I had to pinch myself; all this for free, it was just perfect, and tomorrow tea and an evening with Louise. Which although I was looking forward to immensely also filled me with dread, I knew she would have a welcoming smile, but what would be behind the smile? Was she a different person now, would I still have a place in her heart? In little over twenty four hours I would have those questions answered.

After Friday's settling in and a blissful sleep I awoke to a beautiful May morning. Sunshine, bird songs, in fact all the quintessential calm associated with spring on an English country estate. I was eager yet a little apprehensive at the prospect of going home. For now though I was just content to sit in the sun, enjoy my leisurely breakfast and ponder a while.

I had plenty to plan and get straight in my head, but nothing I couldn't handle.

Every day now, or so it seemed, I was making strides towards my goal. Some strides larger than others, but all in the right direction. I had secured a job with regular hours, domestically we were about to sort out our plan for the future. I had a house at home in Bristol if I needed to go back there to work. I had a cottage on this idyllic estate close to a town with all the amenities I should need. I was finally off the medication. All the boxes in my plan to present a complete package to the authorities were being ticked. I was eager to get down to work and settled so that I could take the next step towards securing custody of the boys.

Driving home I was nervous but excited at seeing Louise. The two hour trip, without motorways, whisked past in a blur of evening sunshine and relaxing green countryside. As I pulled up at the rear of the house my insides were doing cartwheels and by the time I opened the gate to the back garden I was fighting back tears. I hoped and was fairly sure I would get at least a calm and polite reception, but I couldn't be totally certain. I had after all been away for seven weeks on a roller coaster of emotion caused by doing my 'cold turkey' to rid myself of the need for the anti-depressant tablets.

Seven weeks with only the one call home, she stood at the back door just a little distant but as beautiful as ever. A warm smile slowly broke across her face as I walked up the garden path towards her. As expected I was greeted warmly with a softly spoken 'hello' and a polite kiss on the cheek.

Our house was looking lovely; she was a gifted gardener with a real vision, and this being early summer it was in all its glory. In the early part of the year, before leaving for Harrogate, I had built an arbour off the back of the house, which was slowly becoming screened by climbing plants.

The arbour fully covered our large patio with access from the lounge patio doors. I'd fitted external lights too with a vision that we would sit there alone or with friends sipping cold wine on a warm evening. Although we were about to sit and indeed sip cold wine on this lovely warm evening, these circumstances were a million miles from those in the original vision.

Always wary of the need to drive later, as staying wasn't an option, I sipped slowly and very little. The last thing I needed now was to drink and drive. Emotions were strong and positive but they mustn't be allowed to get in the way of the plan.

We ate and we chatted about small things like two people in a very early stage of relationship building. Then, as comfort replaced any awkwardness on either side, we talked and discussed many things well into the early hours. I left before dawn, and although drained with emotion, I felt positive as I drove to Oxfordshire in the emerging sunlight of what was sure to be another lovely day.

Her children were staying and the last thing she needed was awkward questions from innocent mouths. I was missing her before I reached the end of the street.

We knew it would be tight with the two of us, my two and her two. Potentially four teenagers all at the same time! The thought had occurred to us and been discussed that we may need a bigger place. The idea of moving to a larger house was not one that really worried us. We were two professionals with reasonable salaries so we thought it shouldn't be a problem.

I was sad to be leaving our home and Louise, very sad after seven weeks away, and this briefest of reunions. I dearly wanted her to myself but at that moment in time it simply couldn't be.

I arrived back at the cottage in a brilliant sunrise which in all fairness was a bit painful on my tired eyes. I was physically and emotionally drained, yet at the same time confident that all was beginning to come together.

DEVASTATION

Walking very self-consciously through the beautiful grounds of Heythrop Park early Monday morning of the 21st May 2001, the sun already beating down and reflecting in my seriously polished shoes and no doubt off the peak of my cap.

Only the instructors wear caps!

Striding purposely past huge trees, the bases of which were hives of industry for gathering and feeding squirrels, along with the combined chorus of many species of birds, the whole place was alive.

I was fit, strong and ready for the challenge of my new role as a police law trainer. I was also ready for the other battle. How could I fail? I was walking on air. I could actually have done a pretty good job of running through walls; such was my feeling of physical and mental strength.

But why self-conscious?

I had been in police uniform for fifteen years and prior to that in army uniform for eleven years. I was no stranger to bulled (spit and polished) shoes, sharply pressed trousers and shirts. The answer could only be my most recent acquisition, the cap! It was not what it was but more what it symbolised.

Male instructors at the Police Training Centre's all wear

caps, trainee male officers wear the more familiar police helmets, while the women wore a smaller rimmed hat for safety. I felt so proud to wear mine.

As I neared the teaching blocks a fresh faced trainee officer; a young man barely into his twenties walked briskly past me and said, "Good morning staff."

'Staff' was the generic respectful term for the trainers. This greeting was loaded with admiration. I was after all, as were all the qualified police officers, the consummate professionals to which all these trainees aspired.

Nervously at first, I returned this and many more identical greetings with a smile and a "Good morning."

Actually, I quite liked this. My responses, whilst always polite began to vary in form.

Now with a spring in my almost military style walk, the laptop style briefcase swinging along in my left hand, I was beginning to feel pretty darn good. Close to the office and teaching block a sudden wave of terror swamped me, self-doubt and the thought that the smiles I had returned so pompously were just to lure me into a false sense of security.

Like some macabre dream, was I to be put unmercifully to the sword by these angelic faces? I was entering their domain, the classroom. These trainee officers, unlike pupils in a school were all here out of desire to be a police officer. All had endured the tortuous selection process and been kept waiting for a vacancy in some cases for more than a year. Their thirst for knowledge as well as understanding would be immense.

Along with my outer smartness, I now had to deliver the knowledge.

Standing in front of a polished wooden door the confidence and self-importance flooded back. I was standing in front of 'My' office. I had never had an office before, yet alone one with my name on the door.

'Staff G Reed. Avon & Somerset.'

There was another name on there too but it didn't diminish my now extremely important status! Knocking as I entered. What a pillock, knocking on my own door! I could feel myself flush with embarrassment at the thought that the 'angel faces' may have seen that. Inside, I closed the door took my hat off and placed it neatly along with my bag on the empty and, I presumed, my desk.

The door opened again before I had time to settle and in strolled my co habitee, Gary, another Avon & Somerset officer and soon to be training partner. I knew instantly we would get on well, he was carrying two cups of coffee. "Saw you arrive old boy, took a chance on coffee, that ok?"

"Perfect," was my reply. I sat down with my coffee in my office, on my chair – a spinny round one at that. I was aware that the training manager inspector, Mark (South Wales Police) wanted to see me at 8.30am. Having had welcome meetings in the past I set about using the next ten minutes to get as much background on 'the boss' as possible.

Conscious not to say the wrong thing! Gary gave me one piece of advice; do not slag off Welsh rugby.

Even though they were crap at that time, my phraseology at this time would have to be along the lines that they were 'undergoing a period of rebuilding!'

Just before 8.30am a very polite lady breezed into our office, introduced herself and said "The inspector will see you now Geoff."

I reached for my hat but was told that I wouldn't need it.

"We are fairly casual here amongst the staff."

In I walked, and stood behind the desk was Mark, a tall kindly figure with a welcoming smile. Also in the office was another instructor whom I later relied heavily on, he was my development trainer, Graham.

The inspector spoke first, "Geoff I've had a message from your brother in law, can you call this number," handing me a memo.

The number was accompanied on the memo by the words Ashton–under-Lyne Hospital. "You need to make your way to Manchester, I'm afraid your father has not long to go."

Not the welcome I wanted or expected, as he handed me the slip of paper he gestured towards the phone on his desk. After two or three rings it was answered, I introduced myself and was asked to hold. By now I was sweating and shaking with fear.

My sister came on the phone. Quietly, almost whispering "He has just gone Geoff, he's gone."

I heard myself say "Ok."

But I don't recall any more of that conversation, nor even

putting the phone down. My whole world had fallen apart in the time it took to whisper just seven choked words.

Dizzily I struggled back to my feet and along the corridor to my office, on legs about to buckle. Having made it to my office I turned to close the door and was confronted with Graham, unaware that he had followed me from the boss' office.

I reached above his shoulders and pushed the door closed. My legs could take no more. I was suddenly hanging helplessly off him with my arms wrapped around his neck. I was aware of repeatedly sobbing,

"My dad's dead, what do I do?"

I was a lost boy. Where had my voice of reason gone? My source of uncomplicated, almost pragmatic, advice.

By now I was sitting and looking up at Graham. I had made it to my chair and he was perched on my desk. Gary was sat at his desk. Neither knew what to say. The uneasiness was compounded by the fact they had only known me for thirty minutes.

I could see helplessness on their faces and in their eyes. They knew nothing of my history or indeed my determination to secure the boys. Let alone my dependence on my dad.

I knew he was proud of me professionally, I had enjoyed a good military career and within the police service I was doing well. Like all Grandads he loved and was proud of the boys as indeed he was of all his grandchildren.

He was proud of his own military history, having served in

the 11th Hussars. The regiment immortalised in the book and film "The Charge of the Light Brigade."

Instantly I knew I wanted his regimental tie. More than this though and possibly selfishly I dearly wanted him to be proud of me as a man. To see me deal with the trauma of separation, the ensuing custody battle and bringing the boys up to be fine young men. Yes, maybe I did want a lot but I was damn well prepared to fight for it.

Right in that moment though, I was empty, hollow, sitting in the office sobbing unreservedly. I'm one of five children and we had all lost our father that morning. A man not without mistakes, but a man honest enough to admit them.

His eight grandchildren had lost an adoring Grandad.

So in a way I was just one of thirteen children and grandchildren, all now grieving.

Was it as the eldest that I felt compelled to do something? To somehow have answers or reasons, but I had neither. I was wasted. There were others too, our mother albeit long divorced and his present partner. Not to mention his two brothers and their families, as well as a huge number of friends.

As I said earlier in this book, telling the boys that I was leaving was the hardest thing I have ever done. Now, however, was a time that I needed something, some event to hold on to. I needed a handrail to clutch, like on a violently rocking tube train.

I looked back on the vision of lying on the bedroom floor with the boys, all crying but promising mentally to return and get them. From the boys' tears at that point and from my tears of this moment I had to draw strength.

If my dad could have given me one piece of advice before he went I am sure he would have repeated his much proffered line, "I don't care what the bloody hell you do, just look after those lads."

Whenever and wherever this advice was given and through his dower northern accent, love and care spilled from every word.

The boys! How do I tell them? What do I tell them? When do I tell them? What about the funeral?

I needed Louise now, so very much. Should I try to get words to the boys or tell them myself? I had a fabulous relationship with my dad and it was now even more important that, in his memory and for the boy's future that I maintained as good a relationship as I possibly could with the boys.

Yes, I was going for custody, but until I actually make the application to the court and on what specific grounds I hadn't openly discussed this with them. They were still young and I couldn't bear the thought of another piece of uncertainty being thrown into their world. At least once I have made the application I will have some basic answers as to why and when.

'When the time is right, nothing must be left unsaid.'

THE AFTERMATH

"Take as much time as you need Geoff."

I was conscious of Mark next to me and giving me the space I needed. I walked back across the grounds to my house, a beautiful house in a beautiful location but what a difference an hour makes.

The briefcase back in my hand, my cap on my head and neatly cut hair. How different I felt as I retraced my steps, tears rolling freely down my face causing damp spots where they met my pristine white shirt collar.

This was by no means the first time I had cried in uniform. I have seen some horrific things in fifteen years as a policeman. These tears were different ones though; not wholly tears of sadness, not wholly tears of loss. They were tears of sheer determination.

I'm not one who believes that people who have passed away are up there watching. I knew and accepted that my dad had died. I could no longer please him nor could I make him proud. I did however feel a duty to his memory to get the boys safe. A duty built on emotions so strong, coupled with my determination to get the boys, that from now on if you are not with me you had better keep out of my way.

One week later I was starting to accept more fully my father's death.

I had not been allowed to tell the boys directly myself. The legal forces thought it in the boys best interest that I leave the details with them, who could then inform their mother, trusting her to do the necessary. I have to go on record and say that I had absolute faith in my ex-wife to deal with this situation appropriately. She too had a good relationship with my dad.

I do however feel that the legal representatives little twist of ignoring me and taking away the duty I felt I had in telling the boys myself, gave them some form of pleasure.

~

The funeral was horrific, but it was not really going to be anything else.

It had everything from family arguments and falling out to even, unwanted guests. At least my only wish was granted in that I could have dad's regimental tie.

As I arrived at the house it was laid on his bed ready for me. I didn't want to get involved in requests for other possessions. There were many of us wanting different things to remember him by. I suppose it would have been easy to become greedy, even exert a little 'eldest child' pressure but I had some photos, many memories and now his tie.

That day and many times since, I have worn the tie with more pride than I can find words for. Throughout the service, the cremation and the wake I tried desperately to do the eldest son thing.

But I was still a lost boy.

The church service staggered us all. Along with family, and friends that we knew of, the church and indeed the area immediately outside the entrance was packed with folk we didn't know. These were folk that dad had in some way known and they in turn thought sufficient of him to come and show respect.

We were all very grateful to these people.

The cremation service slowly numbed every nerve in my body, as it was always going to. However, as the curtains closed and I realised and accepted that this was the last time I would ever be in the same place with him, I began to shake.

Louise and I were still in the rebuilding stages and although she tried to come with me, she too had children and commitments. She lived in Bristol and the funeral was in Manchester, a round trip of nearly four hundred miles that just wasn't possible in one day.

She simply couldn't be with me. Still she would be there waiting with a warm smile and a hug when I returned. I intended to stay there a few days before getting back to work and resuming the fight.

I stood welcoming people to the wake and dutifully offering drinks. Shame I left it this late to realise it would have been really handy to take some money with me! Fortunately one of Dad's brothers, my uncle and godfather came to the rescue. I had been so wrapped up in my own grief that I struggled with the protocols for the rest of the day.

131

As the final few relatives and friends made their way home and I, totally exhausted both emotionally and physically, began my drive to Bristol.

I hadn't so much as passed Manchester Airport, a little over twenty minutes away when I fell asleep. Only momentarily, but enough to realise that I was never going to make the journey to Bristol; I called my cousin who lived not too far and arranged to spend the night there. Louise fully understood, and half an hour later I was sat with my cousin, who was a real rock for me, pouring my heart out over a large glass of red.

The following day I drove home and spent a few days trying to accept my dad's death as well as convince myself that there was no reason, or blame to be apportioned. No why or wherefore other than straight forward medical reasons.

I was starting to understand my own grief as well as realising that I would get upset at the thought of Dad not being here anymore. Hopefully the tears would reduce as my ability to cope with these moments improved. There were the anniversaries to come over the next twelve months. Fortunately all were in the latter part of the year, both our birthdays in the same week in November, and Christmas and New Year alike in the same December week.

I had six months to get used to him going before I had to deal with those issues. Again I was fortunate in that I had absolutely no doubt that the boy's mum would deal with their grief appropriately.

Once back at Heythrop Park, feeling better by the day and surrounded by some wonderful people, I began to re- emerge as me.

"So let's try again Geoff!" I thought.

Monday morning I walked to work in the sun, the fields, trees, squirrels, same polished shoes and a shiny hat, polite 'Good mornings' offered and returned as I strolled through the stunning grounds again towards my office, and work. Again tears were streaming down my face, but this time not of sadness, nor even determination – sodding hay fever. Is there no let up? My tear ducts must surely need a break!

Late May, almost June and whether I liked it or not it was time to joyfully greet the pollen season. It's grass pollen that does me and here I was strolling pompously through a three hundred acre country estate, what did I expect? Pollen makes me sneeze and squint, while antihistamines make me sleep, so I had long given up on the tablets and instead carried a good supply of tissues and handkerchiefs.

Into the inspector's office I walk, a snotty dribbling mess, manfully trying to explain. I managed to thank Mark for the understanding and time he gave me. He clearly gets the picture that this is hay fever, as a volley of outrageous sneezes threaten the pristine appearance of his gleaming white shirt. Can't think why he didn't offer his hand to shake!

During the first day I was spared any real pressure as I was just introduced to the class I would be teaching with Gary and then left to prepare my lessons, mostly in the office, my office.

Later that day, not only did I have to run the gauntlet of several million pollen particles all seemingly hell bent on getting up my nose as I returned to my accommodation, but I had accepted an invitation to join the other trainers for a drink at the local pub.

A delightful place, with a thatched roof and very English. Once we were all lined at the bar came the polite question; What do you fancy Geoff?" My answer was somewhat pragmatic; "If I could read the beer pumps I would make an informed choice, however I like real ale but can't see, so you choose," offering the responsibility to the guy buying the round.

Suddenly everyone is a doctor. So much advice! Well-meant I'm sure, but all I could think was "how about you lot drink your beer and let me put my head in that ever so inviting ice bucket!"

I had heard that if you eat local honey made with local pollens it lessens the hay fever effect, so applying the 'local' theory to the beer instead of honey, (I made a tenuous link somehow) and proceeded to pour a reasonable but sensible amount of local ale down my throat, always remembering it's work the next day. I don't recall the walk back being so bad so there must be something in that theory.

Three weeks later things were still improving, health, emotion and work. My short, but vicious, hay fever season was finally over.

The improvement was also a very important milestone in

'the plan.' After three two-hour lessons, expert guidance coupled with patient help from Graham, my Trainer Development Officer, my mentor Dan, along with several other trainers, I passed my teaching practice phase.

Now as a qualified trainer I could be thrown into the lion's den alone. I was feeling good again and able to talk about dad. A few tearful moments, but on the whole feeling good.

On the 4th July 2001, Independence Day for American citizens and in support of our US police colleagues we British officers, well at least the training staff at Heythrop chose to celebrate, not that we needed much of a reason, with a barbecue.

It's not difficult in such stunning surroundings to feel enthusiastic about eating and drinking outside. Responsibilities were shared amongst us all, about twenty in total. Gary and I, both ex chefs, set to work on a feast fit for royalty, this was to be no 'burger and sausage' affair. There was cow, deer, fish and bird as well as various breads and salads, as I said, fit for royalty. A group of beer monsters and wine fairies were dispatched to buy out the local village supplies. Not wishing to exclude our non-alcohol drinking colleagues, even signs were put up to show them where the drinking water tap was! A true hoe-down was had by all.

A few hours later I was sitting with others on a friendly patch of lawn, each taking credit for their part in a lovely evening when my phone rang.

"Mr Reed?"

"Yes," I replied "Detective Sergeant (name withheld) from Thames Valley Police here, your son Gavin, (now ten years old) has this evening been taken off your wife and is currently the subject of a police protection order. He is staying with his aunt, Pam. He is well and safe. Please contact me tomorrow to discuss this further."

"Bollocks will I, I want to talk now." I apologised immediately for my language, moved to a much more private location and went on to discuss the situation for some time.

I wandered back towards my accommodation in total disbelief as I listened to the account of that evening's events, some seventy miles away. I felt a surge of anger, deep deep anger that needed to be made productive before it became destructive.

At least he was safe, they both were. I then spoke to their aunt. So grateful that those former spies, whom I viewed with suspicion, were truly acting in the boys best interests now when it was needed. It was time for me to also step up to the mark. I of course knew the police protection order procedure but I wasn't thinking like a police officer now. I was an angry frightened dad. However, even at this raw moment I felt controlled by a hard practical streak.

This was another awful kicking. How many more could I take and still be there for them? I was now terrified that if I got this wrong I would do further damage to their worlds, but doing nothing was simply out of the question. Gavin had obviously been through something really traumatic to now be the subject of a police protection order. I knew that these orders were not used unless absolutely necessary and my mind was spinning out of control with worry. Lewis on the other hand was a little bit older, but, I assumed, had probably witnessed it all. Now he must be feeling desperately alone and terrified for his younger brother. I called their Aunt Pam, and although she was filled with anger and shock she was able, just, to reassure me that Gavin was physically safe, yet very upset and confused. I had no news on Lewis though and no way of contacting him. This was making my stomach churn with worry but I had to stay focused and try desperately to follow the correct path.

My world rocked again, but unlike a few weeks earlier when dad died and I couldn't do anything for him, this time my sons, and in particular Lewis, were in desperate need of me. They needed my help, my devotion, my absolute everything, and this time I really could do something about it.

I walked and talked all the way back to my little cottage, the call finally ended and I sat on a low stone wall gazing at the stars. Yes, through a screen of tears. This was it I thought to myself, the start of the battle. I simply had to succeed; failure was not an option.

There were two confused boys now dependant on me to steady their world. I wasn't angry, I was beyond anger, I was seething, but still strangely calm. I went to bed that night very relaxed. I knew what I had to do and I also knew that I was ready.

UNDERSTANDING THE BATTLE

As all military leaders learn, there are several phases to any battle. Be it a fast and nasty skirmish or a long tactical engagement, the phases are the same. Sadly, as in all battles there are also casualties, sometimes referred to rather impersonally as collateral.

My two beloved sons were the casualties in this battle. Confused, unimaginably saddened at the situation they found themselves in and now separated from the one constant source of support, each other. I had to put that right. I had to get them back on an even keel.

In leaving my wife all those years ago, I felt I had initiated the battle. It didn't, and never would be a moment to look back on with any positive feelings. It was a very sad time and I accept that I will carry a degree of guilt with me forever for the upset I caused. I have learned over the years to deal with this guilt by rationalising it against the fact that I was no longer happy in our marriage and to remain would have potentially made things worse. I accept that guilt, but I don't dwell on it because it can never be positive, for anyone to do that.

Make no mistake about it, it is a battle. Casualties, gains and losses are taken and inflicted by both sides. This is where I come to the whole point of this book. If either parent in similar circumstances believes strongly enough, and for the right reasons, that they are more suited to take on the responsibility for their children's upbringing, welfare and ultimate development, then you simply must never ever give up.

Getting to the point to make the decision to leave and then fight, is however a deep, invasive and painful process. Learning the truth about yourself is ultimately extremely rewarding, but there are without doubt some nasty surprises along the way.

Our children are the biological miracles of my ex-wife and I, both as individuals and collectively. In our case two boys, two people so outwardly different like chalk and cheese. Inwardly they are the same. The same combination of feelings, values and above all emotion brought about their very being.

In the early days they need feeding, changing and nurturing. As they grow the physical demands lessen but the emotional demands increase. Guidance, sometimes firm, is more commonly required as they grow towards adulthood. As any parent will tell you, one of their main emotions and a very powerful one at that is love.

Love and the feeling of being loved during this difficult phase of upbringing for them can feel confusing or broken, not completely broken, more fractured. This fracture needs splinting, supporting and by using any other means appropriate, 'propping up' until a full repair can be carried out.

The warring of their parents is so difficult to understand as is the separation of the two people most dear to them. I know from my own experience that warring parents is a difficult thing to understand. I recall some very sad times as I neared my early teens when my own parents were constantly at each other's throats. If it wasn't about meals being unsatisfactory, then it would be about the time spent in the pub. Regardless of the subject matter it would generally result in a late night argument which I would listen to from the darkness of my bedroom and just wish they would stop. If only they knew how upset we all were upstairs then I'm sure they might have thought a bit more about the effect they were having on me, and my siblings.

I now had to set about repairing this fracture with my own boys. I knew I couldn't return physically, or be on regular speaking terms just yet because the solicitors were doing a good job of keeping me at a distance. I was determined however to show them by whichever means available that my love for them was as strong now as at any other time in their lives.

I tried initially to write this book from a 'non gender specific' angle, based on diaries I had kept, in the hope that I would have answers for my boys when the questions eventually arrived. Not only was I given sound advice that I would fail, but I soon realised for myself, that I can only speak for me.

I can only express my own emotions here. I am a man and more importantly in these circumstances a dad and can only put this across from my point of view. I have tried, as I stated earlier, not to appear as if looking to apportion any blame.

However as events unfold in this, my journey, if any male, female, parent or child draws comparisons with their own lives then I leave it to you and your own values as to whether you form any judgments.

Any parent who feels the strength and depth of love as powerfully as I did, and still do, will recognise instantly that to follow their overwhelming desire to do right for the sake of the children is what really matters.

A thorough and even painful examination of your reasons for fighting will take place. These reasons are the simplest of reasons to feel, but the most difficult to explain and get others, sometimes unwillingly, to accept.

Why do you want custody?

Can you cope with it?

Can you deliver?

If your answers to these questions, and many more you will undoubtedly ask yourself are a clear and honest 'yes,' and the underlying reason is that you love those children beyond words and can do the best for them, then that is the only reason you need. If, however, you have a percentage of desire purely to win and score points over your 'ex' then your reasons in my opinion are wrong. Not only are you doomed for failure, but so much more importantly you will further damage the children.

Never ever use them as pawns in a game. You will ultimately be found wanting and later in life may find yourself facing some very awkward questions, without credible answers.

There are many thousands of families in our society who

break up and the children stay, uncontested, with one or the other parent. I am not for one second attempting to criticise that, more the contrary in that providing the children are safe, loved and aware that they are, is all that matters. The parents in those cases, whether privately sticking pins in effigies of each other or not, are to be praised for putting their children first.

There are various organisations and lobbies that advocate the family unit staying together at all costs and who will continue to make their calls as is their right in our democratic society. I am sure many thousands of parents striving for what is best for their children also have the democratic right to agree with that call. Just as in our democracy there may well be an equal number of committed, caring parents who want to tell them to shut up until they have been in this wholly, unhealthy situation.

The point I am trying to make here and throughout with this book, is quite simply that if you are sure of your reasons, love and resolve, then follow your belief robustly but always accept that you will be challenged many times, as you will exercise your right to challenge others.

Why the in-depth self-assessment, you may ask? The answer is really straight forward. You do it early on in this process in your own domain and in your own time. If you need time to prepare then like all conflicts make sure the preparation is complete before engaging your adversary. You will need time and a great deal of honest realisation if you are to dispel any hidden nasties within yourself whilst in the safety of your own privacy. If you don't do this, I assure you here and now that those opposing you and their advocates will waste no time at all in publicly exposing any weaknesses whether real or perceived.

Ask yourself this one simple question: would you turn up for a marathon without any training?

This will be your marathon, just as it is mine.

CHANGE OF PLAN

Seven am the following morning, after the previous night's sobering conversation with the detective sergeant still ringing and replaying in my ears, I leave the stately beauty of Heythrop Park.

I trundled down to Reading, and ultimately the County Court to apply for an interim residence order for Gavin, a simple process of filling in the required form, which wasn't massive or in depth and paying the requisite sum of money.

Gavin had only been lodged with his Aunt Pam for seventy two hours under the police protection order. This was the maximum period allowed under this order at that particular time. He'd already been there seventeen hours, since the evening before, so there was no time to hang about.

After submitting the application and a multitude of phone calls to social services, solicitors and the like we were listed for a directions hearing the next day.

A directions hearing is where the court listens to your application, decides what the best initial course of action is and allots time to get things sorted, or the process started. Be warned that the time allocated may seem longer than at first necessary but getting the agencies all to speak to each other

144

takes a frustrating amount of time.

I had the support of Karen, our social worker. I had a letter of evidence, a statement if you will from their Aunt and a record of some incidents from school. I was as ready as I could be at that stage. I am used to collecting evidence for court so I wasn't phased about presenting it the following day, but this was so much quicker than I had ever done before.

That night back in leafy Oxfordshire I read everything over and over again. I could be dramatic and say I fell asleep amongst the sea of papers to wake up late, tired and rushing. However that simply is not my style. In a professional and almost dull manner I placed everything in the orange folder in order, marked, cross referenced and highlighted. My clothes were ready, and again I slept well.

The following morning I rose early and arrived at court in plenty of time. I walked into the waiting room and sat confidently chatting to Karen. I have no idea whatsoever where this confidence came from and dearly hoped it was not misplaced. I had by this point been a police officer for some fifteen years and was no stranger to being cross examined, it was an occupational hazard. I had prepared my case as well as I could and was ludicrously calm.

Nothing however prepared me for the walk along the narrow corridor to the judges hearing room. I became dizzy, my legs were shaking and my mouth was suddenly sand dry. I recall looking round at Karen, most probably in panic. She was there just when I needed her with a smile, a gentle hand on my arm and three words, "You'll be fine."

"Yeah, damn right I will," was my whispered reply.

I tried to believe in the legal system, I know I'm right, and for the sake of the boys it has to support me.

Explaining myself in court has become a way of life for me over the years and I realised that my profession has given me a slight advantage over some other parents in this situation. Just be humble and above all honest. I knew the judge wouldn't be some wigged and gowned gargoyle figure, they are human beings.

So many times since these hearings I have spoken to folk who have been through this same process and almost all agree that once you get to the judge it really is just a case of being clear in your requests, your reasons for those requests and your basic plan for the near future as well as long term aims. If you're being honest and what you are asking for is feasible, it will shine through. They purely have to make decisions and judgments based on the law which is already written and even they have to act within, and apply it to the evidence placed in front of them. In doing so, the best interests of the children are served.

My second point here is one of caution though: they are very intelligent and experienced professionals. They will have already come across every possible lie, devious tactic or self-interested ploy imaginable. Trust me, if you try any of these they will see right through you instantly and make an already tough ordeal, purgatory. Even with right on your side you have

146

to be clinically honest otherwise you risk damaging the children by your failure.

So, a large meeting table, a grey suited gent at the head of it and a few books on the desk in front of him. Just a few books, not a library built to impress. More importantly an open file, evidence that my application has been read, in such stressful situations, even with experience it is bizarre the things you do remember and ones you don't. I can recall the yellow file-folder lying open, across the middle of his desk and an opened fountain pen resting in the centre crease of the file. I can't however recall who was sat across the table from me.

Opening shots to me, as it was my application; I was unnaturally calm. Having worried about what it would be like, that worry was now gone, I was living it. I was in it for real. I have, for obvious reasons to be careful what I recount of the court proceedings. Suffice to say I explained why I made the application for this interim residence order, which was in place now for Gavin, and what I wanted from this court now and in the future.

I spoke slowly giving reasons for everything. Preparation was so important at that stage. There is no mileage in gorging on unpleasant detail. My dignity and that of the boys is paramount. After my explanation a voice from the other side of the table responded. I cannot recall any particular words nor too many objections, but I knew they would come later. My only moment of real panic was when the judge turned towards me with an icy stare and said,

147

"How long will all your enquiries take" and then with air of almost menace he added, "And remember this is about the children, let's not delay."

I looked helplessly at Karen, I simply had not considered being put on the spot like this. She spoke with calm professionalism,

"Two months should be sufficient Sir."

"Very well," he said, "4th October it is, wait at the Court office for your papers."

Wow, that was it, ten minutes. Gavin was safe at his Aunt Pam's for two months. I had a lot to do but I placed trust and the boy's well-being in Karen's hands. I had no doubt about her ability, or my determination.

I had to arrange suitable accommodation for us all at Heythrop Park or return home to Bristol, and if that was the case then what role can I fulfill back in the force? I had also to inform Gavin's school and take them a copy of the order before the end of the day. Lewis, the elder son was not subject to the Interim Residence Order, nor had he been included in the police protection order but he was still equally a part of my heart as well as my application for custody of them both.

I had much to do and couldn't wait to get started. This was it; this was what I had been trying to prepare for, all the hills in Scotland and all the miles on the bike. Sad that my dad wasn't still around and even though he had only passed seven weeks earlier he had to be put aside until October. I didn't think that he would mind.

Clutching the forms I would need in the near future, a copy of the order duly delivered by a court office usher, and the promise that a letter detailing the exact time on the 4th October would be forthcoming, I walked out of the air conditioned court into the stifling July heat. I now had interim custody and as such did not need any reason or excuse to see Gavin. Lewis was still living with his mum and contact with him was to prove problematic and produce much heartache, but I had to deal with it.

The big picture, as I saw it, was ultimately the three of us together and no restrictions on contact with either of them, and I had to hang on to that. I hadn't seen either of the boys for some weeks. My efforts had been frustrated one way or another. I was desperate to see them and to hold them, to reassure them that my love for them was still as strong. The reality of the situation was that my love was not only as strong but now driven by passion.

I rang the schools. Lewis's was a little distant with me at first being under the misconception that there was a court order against me. I put them right on a few things, and when at the threat of legal action they admitted they had not actually seen an order, I insisted Lewis be allowed to call me or Karen whenever he wished. And woe betide them if I found out that he had not been allowed this right. I had sensed just a sniff of advantage shifting slightly towards me, and without charging away like a snowball down a mountain I felt the steep incline in front of me had been reduced to almost level.

149

Being a big bloke with cycling and hill-walking as hobbies, uphill was always a bit of a struggle, but on the flat or downhill and with steadily gathering momentum I was a formidable opponent. This was flat enough for me now.

I rang Gavin's school in Wokingham, staffed by wonderful, caring people. As I explained the situation the voice from the other end calmly said to me,

"Why not just pop in and see him, he would love to see you."

"Yes I will... I can," was my faltering reply.

After a few moments I remembered that I can do that now without groveling to all and sundry for permission.

"I'll be there in half an hour."

Soon I was parking my car, my trusty old Rover in the school car park. I walked into the school office, nervous, excited, yet terrified. I simply didn't know how Gavin would react. What had he been told of why he was in this awful position? It was testimony to the all-round sadness of our situation that I was questioning my own son's potential reaction to me.

"Ah, Mr. Reed, perfect timing" was the greeting from the ever cheerful staff, "Just in time, he is with his class on the field at the back of the main house, just go round, his teacher is aware you're on your way."

Gavin on the other hand had not been informed. As I walked around the main house in beautiful tree shaded grounds I could hear my heart pounding. Kicking its way through what appeared to be a very flimsy ribcage. I emerged into the bright sunlight on the corner of the playing field. After a few seconds and a little prompt from his teacher, Gavin turned, looked for a second and then saw me. I had always believed I was right to pursue this course but if I needed any more convincing then this was the moment.

I raised my hand in a high five style gesture but didn't walk forward any more. He stopped what he was involved in and began sprinting across the field towards me.

"Daaaaaaaaaaaaaaaaad" was the continuous bellow he let rip as he ran. Blonde hair, white shirt, grey shorts and grey socks. His shoes were black but a mere blur against the grass. As he neared me my eyes flooded and my throat hurt so much in trying to choke back the tears. I began to crouch a little and then "THUD" his chest hit mine. I felt his head on my shoulder and his arms lock around my neck. In this instance I felt wholly vindicated and knew that to have pursued any other course would quite frankly have been pure neglect.

This was witnessed by other staff who whilst trying to contain a group of ten olds, were also wiping the odd tear.

After a while hugging, crying and eventually chatting I left him at the school with a promise to collect him on Friday and take him to my country mansion for the weekend!

The court order clearly stated that he should reside with his Aunt Pam during the week and she still had the casting vote over where he spent the weekend.

My ex-wife, his mum had restrictions placed over her

level of contact, whilst I on the other hand had no such restrictions and looked forward with confidence to being a 'full-on' dad once again.

I drove back to Heythrop Park, exhausted but happy, and although it was after teatime when I arrived, food was the last thing on my mind. In the office wing that evening I bumped into my supervisor, a lady called Frances. Frances could immediately see the strain clearly evident on me and just at that moment gave me the hug I needed, and I was happy to accept.

After much discussion that evening and indeed the following morning it was very clear that I would not, to my huge disappointment, be able to reside on the estate with the boys. Schooling was one of many measures, as was the appropriateness of the boys living in shared grounds with only adults and no other children. Much as I was deeply disappointed at the prospect of having to leave Heythrop I had started a process which I believed would ultimately bring Gavin, Lewis and I back together full time. The location whilst important was not the main factor.

Later the following day, after basically a whole day of discussion and phone calls it was agreed to delay my submitting a notice to return to my own force until after the hearing on 4th October. There were other housing options available or maybe even a transfer to Thames Valley Police, and live near them. Potentially catastrophic for my relationship with Louise, and one I would only take as a last resort.

It was now Thursday night and I eagerly awaited Friday to

see Gavin again and bring him to Heythrop. I was also aware that he would ask lots of questions and whilst I had to be honest about my intentions I also had to manage his expectations, and those of Lewis, very carefully. So vivid are the recollections as I go through the process of writing this my eyes filled with tears again.

The following morning Frances arrived for work early and immediately invited me into her office. She was a very active person, asking only short questions and indeed expecting only short answers.

"Do you know where Bramshill is?"

"No" I answered.

Frances informed me it was ten miles at the most from the boy's schools. A police college which I had heard of, but not visited was there and they have an initial training wing, just like this one where I was now working.

"If they found you a flat or house for you and the boy's would you work there instead of here?"

"Yes." I replied resoundingly.

"Ok, go there now, it is just south of Reading, see Inspector Julie. Let me know what you think."

This interaction – hardly a conversation, lasted no more than a minute but was a moment of generosity and kindness that will live with me forever. I hope to be able to find Frances one day and thank her in person. In short she and Julie were longtime friends both now running and working in training establishments.

Two hours later I pulled into Bramshill Police College, and was stunned. What a spectacular place, another country estate comprising of four hundred acres of woodland, lakes and fresh air. A country house also steeped in history close to the Hampshire village of Hartley Wintney. The difference being that it was a long established police centre with many families living within the grounds. Finally finding Julie's office I was greeted with a warm smile and what I presumed was an air of sympathy. I later discovered this to be in fact empathy.

I was again to be taken aback by the well-meaning and wholly unassuming folks I was now working amongst. In reality I didn't know many of them but here I was a stranger being given monumental help. Julie handed me a Yale key and on the brown tie-on label was written an address.

"Go and have a look, it's available now but if it's not suitable you may have to wait a little longer for something bigger."

I was stunned. A little over seventy two hours since being granted the order giving me until 4th October and here I was on my way to view a potential home for the three of us.

After a short walk I was climbing the echoing concrete stairs to a second floor flat. I couldn't help but notice even before I went in that it was surrounded by grass areas and overlooking a beautiful lake. Was this really happening?

I let myself in and began the tour; the kitchen was fitted and fairly new with all white goods, crockery, cutlery and even a kettle and microwave. The lounge was huge, a three piece suite, dining table and chairs and welsh dresser. French windows obviously fitted with safety railings looking out onto more grass and trees. There were even a few decorations around the place. The bathroom was good, with shower and I will spare you a description of the loo. It was what it was, but more importantly clean and tidy.

The whole place was fitted with carpets. It was perfect. I stood looking at the twin beds for a moment and couldn't help picturing the boys asleep in them. For a brief moment it all became just a little too much for me. This was happening so fast and how I hoped that I wasn't dreaming. I sat on one of the beds and cried. This truly would be perfect.

After a brief tour of the work areas I gave Julie my answer: a very grateful yes. I would love to work and bring the boys up there.

Later that afternoon I made the short ten mile journey and collected Gavin from school, but sadly was having trouble getting to Lewis. I knew barriers would be put in place. I also knew he was being put under pressure. I had already, in the early days of this struggle, decided that as difficult as it was and as much as I ached to see him I would not try to put pressure on him, or either of them from my side too.

I couldn't bear the thought of them growing up in an ever tightening vice. E-mail and phone contact I would use to reassure him that I was there should he need me.

As Gavin and I made our way to Heythrop I agonised over what to tell him. He was a bright inquisitive boy who had sadly had his world turned upside down. If I was to truly begin to stabilise his life, and him, I would need to answer his questions honestly. What I could not and would not do though was to raise his hopes by prejudging the court result. That weekend at Heythrop as well as packing to move to Bramshill, I started to explain to him what I was trying to do, how I had to go about it and that it simply wouldn't happen quickly. I also had to try and prepare him for the deep and somewhat searching nature of the Social Services and CAFCASS (Children And Families Court Arbitration Service) enquiries that were about to begin.

I couldn't get to Lewis. But I hoped that if I explained it to Gavin, he would in turn tell his brother. I tried to explain that as well as being the centre of the enquiry both boys had an extremely important role.

Knowing that their loyalties to me, and their mum would be stretched to the very limits in the coming weeks, all they had to do was tell the truth to whoever was asking them questions. I tried to round this preparation off by explaining that his mum, Karen from Social Services and I would not allow anybody to ask them anything unless they had their best interests at heart.

As for the move to Bramshill, well that was simple to explain. Gavin knew that I was applying for custody and that Bramshill was only a short distance from his school. I also tried to be open about the prospect about not getting custody, in which case I was nearer, so it would be easier for visits.

By mid Aug 2001 the process of collecting evidence for the October hearing was gaining momentum. The saying 'when

156

the going gets tough' was very much the case now. Karen and her social services department were putting together the required papers. Much of the content I had been hither to unaware of.

I swung daily from sadness to downright horror and fury. Sometimes having to re-read the documents if only to justify my reaction. I was usually fully justified. As you can imagine I cried often but always spurred on by my driving desire to get the boys to what I considered to be a place of emotional safety. I tried never to ease the pressure on the professionals on whom I was so dependant.

ALL STAND

Monday, two weeks later and it's my first day at work in the initial training wing at Bramshill Police College. Showered, breakfasted. Smart in my uniform, shiny shoes and I picked up my cap, without touching the peak which would have unsightly finger smudges on it! I couldn't help recalling last time I reported for work for the first day. I thought of my dad. A tear welled up and spilled onto my cheek.

I missed him so much. I still can't find words to describe my feeling of loss. I believe that had he still been alive I think he would have been pleased with me so far, and that was reassuring. I strode out into the sunshine, dodged the geese, and walked into the office. I sat a while at another 'me' desk and even placed an order form for stationary, I was feeling so important!

After a few welcoming words from the training manager I was introduced to a guy who was to become an integral part of my development as a trainer, and a constant source of support over the next couple of years. I am delighted also to say that John and his lovely wife Sarah are close personal friends to this day. I was honoured in September 2007 to become their daughter Freya's God parent.

John was a trainer I was to work with, and to my physical detriment, drink with on several occasions over the next three years. For some unknown reason when sufficiently refreshed on Old Thumper, wonderful real ale from his home town brewery Ringwood, he all too often saw the need to show me the finer points of prop forward scrummaging. I have loved playing rugby but never delved into the dark world of the front row!

Life began to settle a little. I was seeing plenty of Gavin but sadly very little of Lewis. I knew Lewis was battling with divided loyalty. He was loyal to his mum and I respected that, I was able to chat on the phone from his aunt's, plus a few emails and even a couple of priceless meetings, again at his aunt's. I knew the pressure he was under and I continued to stick to my decision not to put him under equivalent pressure from my side.

I was satisfied that he knew I loved him with all my heart and soul, and although not trying to kick down doors to get to see him regularly as yet, I was working hard in the background.

I and the flat were visited many times by various departments of the Social Services, CAFCASS and the police over the coming weeks.

Finally by mid-September, with Gavin back at school, the leaves were beginning to fall and the air outside as chilling as the mood. The 4th October hearing wasn't far away. Much as I despise solicitors and indeed the whole of the civil legal system. I heeded the advice being continually offered and took to the streets of a nearby town to find a solicitor, eventually finding one sympathetic to my cause and optimistic enough to take me on as a client.

There was simply no way, even allowing for the obscene amount of money taken each month by the Child Support Agency, would I qualify for legal aid. I feel repulsed at the way the system works on determining how legal aid is allocated.

It may be a pipe dream but what a wonderful idea to rid society of the money and power crazed solicitors and barristers and maybe replace them with 'common sense and reason commissioners.' It's a nice dream.

Anyway, having found a solicitor I felt Ok with, I relate my situation to this individual who makes copious notes and plenty of 'hmm, hmm, hmm' type noises.

Leaving the office and making my way home I have a deep feeling of unease. Why should I trust this guy? He doesn't know me, or the boys. He doesn't know anything except what I have managed to get across in that very swift half hour. I guess my real problem is that I didn't trust him to fight with me. He may well know the law as it stood, but would he be prepared to challenge it. Challenging established practices and procedures is the only way to tell if they are still relevant in today's fast moving and changing society. I didn't want some establishment lap dog to just eloquently speak about my virtues as a person. I needed almost a maverick; a fighter to firstly believe that the boys were better off with me and then fight for that.

I accept that I was all consumed by love, passion and my honest belief and that no solicitor was going to match my drive, but a little fire in the belly would have been an encouraging sign. Even now as I write this I get strange feelings of vulnerability again in relation to that particular time. I had become reliant on people, professional people who were filling me with confidence by their belief in my goal, such as Karen, but others, like this guy, weren't. Maybe it says a lot more about me, in that I was uncomfortable and vulnerable relying on folk without this belief. Could I trust them? Would I ever trust anyone again? Who knows?

As the weeks progressed and the date for the hearing grew ever closer, the meetings became more frequent. Some I felt good about, some I didn't. Karen filled me with hope. I always looked to her meetings for realistic, sensible support and guidance. She always delivered. I don't think I could ever amply repay her. She only had the boy's welfare at heart. She was un-fluffy, but had a quiet sincerity about her. I really trusted her.

CAFCASS; the arbitration service were represented by a totally different lady. After the original meeting in her office in Oxford, I recall she visited me a couple of times at the flat in Bramshill; once with Gavin there, and at least once without either of the boy's present. The visits without them were much more an inspection and interview. 'Show me this, show me that. Where will they stay? How will they get to school? Can you cook? Can you iron? Can you run a home? What will you do for holidays?'

This kind of attention to detail filled me with confidence. There was even a question or two in relation to my health. I was so pleased that I had stopped taking the anti-depressants. In fact the opposite, it was so good to explain that I had needed them in the past, got off them once they were no longer required, and free from any regular medication. I also took pleasure in explaining I had now gone two years without cycling head first into any walls or under buses!

This lady, as part of her role was in the process of speaking to all people involved, even the boys independently. She would gain their views, and finally submit a report which would be hugely influential in the Judge's eventual decision. With this in mind, I was so careful not to appear, despite unbelievable provocation, vindictive. If I showed even a sniff of my application for custody being a method to score points over the boy's mum, instead of genuinely believing I was better suited to bring them up, the application would be over. There and then.

Not once in all the meetings, discussions, or even interviews, did I come over that way. I had examined myself deeply and honestly before I began this process, but like a lot of things your true feelings can only be tested fully in the real situation. This was very real, I was right about myself and it felt very good.

The agreement with the solicitor was to wait until the CAFCASS report was finalised and submitted before we met again to discuss the plan for court. I wasn't happy with that idea at all, although I accepted that we would need to see the report prior to the hearing. Surely though 'we' should have a plan before and if needs be, adapt as required. I was growing more and more frustrated with the legal process. Wait, wait, wait, I kept telling myself. So I waited and a week or so before the court date, the CAFCASS lady duly arrives with the report. I just knew that there would be something in there that was going to hurt. The report was in a thick document file. The views of all concerned.

"Ninety percent positive," was her opening line as she began to tell me about it in summary before leaving me to read it. "Social services are totally behind your application. The boy's aunt is also totally behind you."

Ok, Ok I get the picture, I thought – but who is the ten percent against? I was desperate to know.

My ex-wife of course! She is bound to disagree whole heartedly with anything I suggest, but that was to be expected. After all, I would probably disagree with anything she had to suggest. That's just the way it goes, I suppose.

"It's Lewis," I went dizzy as she spoke.

My lounge was spinning and I felt instantly sick. I could feel the tears on my face again. I had been the one ascending, but now I could feel myself tumbling, out of control for a while. It's not supposed to go like this. Help me, someone please help me.

I was aware of her trying to tell me that there was a good reason. How? I wasn't arguing with her, just struggling to grasp the situation. After a few moments, having settled and become more receptive, I began to take in what she was saying. As it was explained to me I bizarrely began to feel a very different form of pride. Lewis was the eldest of the boys, but even so, only thirteen. Already he was able to identify, amid all this emotion and possibly confusion, what is important to him. The things that matter in his life and his world. He hadn't bowed to pressure from any angle. I was so proud of him and the resilience he was already showing. There I was, fighting like a man possessed for the welfare and wellbeing of the two people most precious to me, and both of them were individually showing me that already they had strength of characters beyond their years.

Gavin, was showing strength beyond his years and an incredible understanding of his situation. As parents we should be continually amazed by the fortitude displayed by our children, sometimes in extreme adversity. This I saw with my own eyes, albeit via a CCTV link, when Gavin spoke so clearly and accurately when he was interviewed by specialist police officers earlier that year. Lewis, in another way by his decision based on his wishes in the face of overwhelming pressure. Pressure not from any one person but pressure brought on by the dilemma of trying to see through the fog of emotions affecting his life.

The exact same strength I was trying to sustain now. Were they showing me exactly what I was hoping to show my dad, if he were still here? I think they were, albeit without realising.

I recall so clearly, eventually going to bed that night after ploughing through much of the CAFCASS report. I lay in bed with a cocktail of tears flooding my eyes, blurring the moon and surrounding stars as I gazed out of the window. Some stayed in my eyes, some ran down my face. I didn't mind crying. I needed to be honest with myself, as well as others. The tears were a mixture, some of deep sadness at Lewis's choice, some were pride at his resilience. Some sadly were from resultant realisation that in a week's time the judge may separate the boys! Not growing up together wasn't the plan. The coldness of the wet pillowcase reminded me, as I lay staring out of the window at the moon, that I was still extremely worried.

A day or so later and it was time to visit the solicitor. I sat, dumbfounded, in the plush offices looking at this very well groomed individual. I listened intently as he explained that he had, on my behalf and at a cost of several hundred pounds already, instructed and sought advice from the barrister. Every word was precise, in its meaning and delivery, quoting act and section from various legal documents. Whilst I wholly accepted that under the Children's Act the views of both boys would be of paramount importance in the final report from CAFCASS, which would greatly influence the final decision in court, I simply could not, and would never accept that my goal would have to change. Not now. Not less than a week from the hearing. Not ever. I could feel the anger and frustration boiling inside me.

Like listening to a politician when asked for a simple yes or no, this stripe-suited man simply was not prepared to challenge the law. He was so wrapped up in case-law which only looks backwards, that he simply couldn't, or wouldn't fight for the boys in the manner I wanted and needed him to. He started to suggest that I drop the application for custody because one of the boys had chosen to remain with his mother for his own reasons and therefore the younger one would not be placed with me.

This individual wanted me to go for unrestricted access, which would undoubtedly be granted along with a variety of safety measures. He had completely lost sight of the issue. Gavin had been placed under a police protection order, lodged with his aunt temporarily and had been on the social services child protection register. He simply wasn't safe. He had ADHD and as such was difficult to handle at times. I had realised whilst researching my own past that I had been similar as a child. Although not diagnosed back in the sixties, I just got regularly slapped as class 'bad boy.' Detention was my after school club. I was intelligent, very quick to learn but tended to roam around class like a grenade looking for somewhere to explode.

Using my intelligence, and indeed instinct I quickly decided I had to do something about the solicitor. Initially recruited as someone to assist me, he was beginning to become a hindrance. I suppose it's to the credit of the court system, that I have condemned throughout my journey, that it allows me to present my case myself. I may not be as eloquent and learned as he and his type but as with all people fighting for something they are passionate about, I had a fire in my belly that would shine through when it mattered.

I was fast approaching the time when I was to be really tested as to my desire and my belief. If I had left any stone unturned, then this was to be the moment I would find out.

Back to the solicitor; extreme physical violence wasn't really an option. Much as I would have liked to have put him through his expensively decorated wall, and believe me I was so angry I would have been capable of it but, applying for custody of my sons was going to be difficult enough without being on an assault charge. Nor was it a good career move!

Instead I chose to write: 'I'll do it myself, send me your bill,' on a piece of paper and slide it under his nose. By the time he had read it I was heading for the door. No shouting or swearing, it's not my style. Down the stairs, along the streets seething with anger I drove back to Bramshill.

My brain was doing cartwheels as I began to think through the task I had just set myself. I knew it would be a daunting task, even with my comfort within the court environment. I was however determined to face this head-on. I simply could not go into court with any other attitude, nor could I rely on people with less belief. I spoke again at length with the CAFCASS lady. I had no regrets about getting rid of the solicitor, but I think she was a little wary of my ability to represent myself against a barrister for my ex-wife. Karen I believe was a little uneasy too, but given my profession, didn't really offer any objection and just advised caution. I knew I could count on

CAFCASS and Karen as to the law. I knew the content of the various reports, and without being arrogant I was confident that I was in the right. I hadn't had, as was required by the court process, any reports or evidence attacking my suitability as a dad or a potential single-parent. I just had to keep focused on the team representing my ex-wife, making sure that they didn't de-rail me with any deft moves or slimy smiles.

The night before court Gavin was at his aunt's. He didn't need to know what was happening. He was ten, and although he was showing remarkable resilience and acceptance of his situation, he didn't need to know any more at this stage. The future would yield the answers. I sat well into the evening, checking, rechecking and rehearsing my opening speech. I knew that I had to start off well, positive but not too aggressive, eloquent but not too rehearsed. Whilst clear and concise I still had to be coming from my heart. I made sure the reports were cross referenced and notes, where needed, made in margins.

Trying to make sure all would be in order; my preparations had to go beyond the paperwork. What shall I wear for court? I am a very informal person and the only suit I had was a dinner suit, which wasn't quite right. I wasn't about to turn up like an overdressed Christmas turkey. No; I just had to be me. Smart jeans, blue shirt and brown shoes. I needed to present the real me. The caring, loving, driven father; only concerned about the boy's wellbeing. Many hundreds of times over my years as a police officer, when asked by worried witnesses before court, I would say just wear what you feel comfortable in. Be tidy but also just be you. So I did exactly that, for once I actually took my own advice. Eventually, with clothes ready and evidence all sorted, I sat down to enjoy a large-ish glass of red. Feeling strangely calm I knew I was as prepared as I possibly could be.

A little over twelve hours later at Reading County Court on a dank October morning I sat in a small consulting room with the lady from CAFCASS and Karen discussing how I was to present the case. The basic plan was that I begin; I'd give an overview of relevant dates and events so far, followed by why I wanted custody, concluding with my suitability as well as the arrangements I had already put in place and the forward planning I had been able to do should the court decide in my favour. CAFCASS and Karen would then individually answer questions in relation to the reports submitted. It was very difficult and indeed dangerous to try and second guess the court, but it was a way of staying focused so my mind was blocking out anything other than what may be about to happen, and my possible response.

'Tap, tap' on the door, and a suited individual entered and enquired 'as to counsel.' I re-stated that I was presenting my own case. A fact he should have been fully aware of. I instantly felt nothing but utter contempt for this individual who, I believed was my ex-wife's legal representative, her barrister, and would soon be offering the court a stream of pathetic excuses. Trying to defend the indefensible. I could do no more than look him straight in the eye.

Throughout all my training, many years' experience and,

the training I now give to new recruit officers, one word is continually used when explaining the legal system in England and Wales: ADVERSARIAL. In a nutshell, each side present a case to the court which the other side are allowed to cross examine and try to break down by a polite but exhaustive process of questioning. Once both sides have placed their case, and had an opportunity to cross examine the other side's case, including all personal witnesses as well as paperwork and reports, the judge or whoever will eventually decide the case and will make a decision. The judgment.

In the majority of cases all the paperwork must be submitted in good time for the opposition, and more importantly the judge, to read prior to the hearing and have a good knowledge of the issues. In fact judges take a very dim view of last minute evidence being thrown into proceedings.

"Do we have anything to discuss?" asked the suited individual.

What a bizarre question. I think he was offering me the opportunity to ask him for a compromise and therefore handing him the moral high ground from which he could offer me a 'very generous' compromise and therefore obtain an advantage in the eyes of the court.

He was now, by this very reasoning, clearly my adversary. I had therefore, no feelings for him. No professional etiquette. He stood between me and the safety of my boys. I had no desire to talk to him, I was raging inside and the last thing I needed were his slimy words ringing in my ears. I was wholly and dangerously out of my depth when it came to in-depth family legal issues. I knew that if it came to arguing a point of law, he would tie me in knots, but I truly believed I had right as well as the law, on my side.

"Have you read my application?" I asked in reply to his initial question.

"Yes" before he could say anything else, I continued, "Have you read the reports?"

"Yes" was his reply.

"Then I have nothing to say to you." was all I could muster by way of polite response.

I was on the edge of survival now and needed to rely heavily on my experience in courtroom procedure:

1. Never get involved in an argument with a solicitor in court.

2. Keep your emotions inside; difficult as it would be in these circumstances.

3. Give short answers: 'yes' or 'no' if possible thereby giving them little or nothing to seize upon and lead you astray.

After he had left the room I sat down and looked at the CAFCASS lady and Karen, both were smiling gently, but what percentage of those smiles were sympathy? What percentage anxiety? I didn't know and it was too late to ask.

"The case of Reed v Reed" boomed out of the public address system.

We all filed in. This time not the small office style courtroom, but a more traditional layout just smaller in size. I was, however, grateful for a much shorter walk than the last court hearing. The judge's seat clearly at the front, high above and looking down at the rest of us. We were all ushered in and instructed to swiftly take up our positions, like a silent run through of an intricate group dance, then remain standing until the judge had taken up position. There was the obligatory sounds of feet and chairs being shuffled which quickly subsided to hushed whispers followed by silence. The stage was now set.

I had decided not to look at my ex-wife or any of her representatives. The courtroom was simple in that it was about ten rows of seats each served by a continuous desk either side of a central aisle. I stood at the front left seat and bench, and my adversary at front right, poles apart in many ways.

The judge entered swiftly and with very little ceremony stood in front of his chair. We bowed swiftly yet respectfully, with little more than a nod of the head, us toward the judge and him in turn, towards us, then we all sat.

The judge informed the court that he had read in depth all the evidence submitted, and asked was there any further information to present that he hadn't yet seen, or changes in the position of either party.

A nervous, "No Your Honour" I heard myself croak.

Then, as the applicant, I was invited to stand. I remember all the eyes burning into me.

In truth I didn't speak much. I simply informed his honour that I was self-represented and was still asking the court for custody, although I did appreciate that Lewis had exercised his right under the relevant law and expressed his wish to continue residing with his mother as he had valued friends and a developing social circle. A decision I respected and although I was fundamentally opposed to it I would in no way try to alter or influence him in the future.

Gavin, on the other hand was too young, and extremely vulnerable given the ordeal he had undergone and the circumstances he finds himself in. I was willing and able, more able than his mother in my opinion, to provide the loving, stable home life he needed and deserved.

Just when I was starting to relax and work methodically through my notes the judge interrupted my flow,

"Thank you Mr Reed, please sit down."

But I hadn't finished. Had he heard enough?

"Mr Reed, please sit."

"Oh yes, sorry Your Honour." I was terrified, so entranced that I had forgotten to sit down!

I listened intently as my adversary began to wax lyrical about the reasons for children remaining with the mother in such cases and the effects of siblings being separated. Furthermore, the pressure of separation on the mother.

Then a thought occurred that they must have some low ballers to throw in at the last possible moment. Then again, no because they should have made that known when the judge asked for any more information at the start of the hearing. My head was spinning. Then, after winding up to a heartfelt plea based on the impossible, he sat down. By impossible I mean

173

that Gavin had been taken off his mum, so clearly couldn't be placed back in her care.

Oh my god, that's all they had. No wonder the barrister was trying to get me to ask for a compromise.

"Mr Reed do you have anything further?" said the judge.

I stood again and passionately, but without waffling, just reiterated that I accepted that the issue of siblings being separated (I already felt this was about to happen) was far from ideal. I still firmly maintained, however, that as both boys were on the child protection register as a consequence of past issues, the subject of their future safety was the greater issue here. I concluded by re-stating that I had to accept the findings of the reports and had anticipated those reports having a greater bearing on the court's decision, but I believed still that that issue would be best resolved by both residing with me.

I had made my point clearly, from the heart but without trying to misuse emotion. The judge will have seen and heard it all before, and although the boys were priceless to me, we were all just another case number to him. He wasn't to be swayed at this late stage.

I sat down, immediately; I had done all I could. I felt a comforting pat on my left upper arm from behind. I knew it was the CAFCASS lady. I knew I had done right. I knew I had given everything I had. I was sweating, shaking and almost incapable of pouring and drinking a glass of water. I just kept thinking of that awful moment, years ago, crying on the bedroom floor telling the boys I was leaving, and sobbing with them. I could see them both in confusion and dis-belief, as I promised to come back for them. Now here I was desperately trying to honour my promise yet the final decision was not mine. My anchor had held incredibly firm over all these years and the process was to culminate in this room within the next few minutes.

After what seemed an age, the silence was broken by the Judge's voice. A short preamble in relation to which law he had used in reaching his decision.

Then his decision: "I make the order that Lewis reside with the respondent mother and have unrestricted access to his father and that Gavin reside with the applicant father. The court would deliver copies of the written order via the court office."

A few closing words, then he stood up and left as swiftly as he had entered less than half an hour earlier. We all stood and bowed.

As the judge left the room my feelings were a strange but heady mixture. In there somewhere was satisfaction, but I was numb and dizzy for a few seconds. It was as if I was looking over a very steep cliff and although I knew I wasn't going to fall, I felt anxious. I didn't feel too steady on my feet either, as if I'd stood up too quickly and got a bit of a head rush.

After what was probably only a few seconds, but felt like I had been standing motionless for an age with everyone looking at me, I quickly gathered my things from the desk and bolted from the courtroom, to the sanctuary of the consultation room. I was nearest the door and didn't want to hear any unpleasant comments if my adversary and her group were to pass.

In the little room, I thanked and hugged the ladies who had helped me so much, who had believed in me, in what I was and my efforts for the boys. We all shared tears – a good tear moment.

After a few moments I made my way to the court office counter and collected my copy of the order. After reading it several times I made my way out of the building. I walked into the busy street, folder under my arm just as I had arrived, well almost, there was one extra piece of paper in the folder!

I had done it. Gavin was safely in my custody and Lewis, although still with mum as he wished, there were measures allowed within the order that would hopefully allow frequent and regular contact. I thought at this stage I would have been crying for England.

No I was too damn hungry and thirsty so I headed straight for the buffet at Reading railway station. I got the largest pasty available to mankind and a large cup of strong coffee, sat down and devoured them. Still not crying, nor was I laughing or even smiling; just drawn, exhausted and fully vindicated.

All around me were folk going about their lives, unaware of the real life drama I had just been part of. I wondered, were any of these folk in the position I was three years ago. Don't ever give up.

I sat and thought for many hours over the coming few days as to why it seemed to be over so quickly and can only believe that if the preparation is right then the conclusion, with little or no room left to manoeuvre will be swift. By that I mean I was fully prepared physically as well as mentally – looking and feeling fit and strong, no obvious weaknesses and no unnecessary medication; emotionally I opened myself up and really questioned my motives. You cannot win if the motive is wrong, you will be exposed and more importantly risk further emotional damage to the children. I'd been tested to the core and beyond it, even deeper. I found my anchor, buried it deep and fought like someone possessed.

HOMEMAKER

I called their Aunt Pam to thank her for all her support including her letter supporting my application. I arranged to collect Gavin from school and tell him on the way home. She was to help me massively over the coming three years, as a child minder for Gavin on a daily basis before and after school depending on her shifts.

It was great help to Gavin too in settling things down after the turbulence of the last few months. She and her husband would also take Gavin for the odd weekend so that Louise and I could have some quality time together.

Louise, yes, still at home a hundred miles away, trying to support me. Giving me all the support I asked for, and more importantly the support I didn't ask for but was clearly visible to her that I needed. She was there Friday afternoons when we arrived home; she was there in my rear view mirror, albeit a little blurred, as we drove away Sunday afternoons. I so looked forward to getting home to see her, to hold her and generally be near her. Did she feel the same? I think so, but something was wrong. Was my working away turning our relationship into a weekend romance? Maybe that was all I was prepared and indeed able to give at that time.

My heart ached just to see her. I recall one New Years Eve in fancy dress standing on the rear lawn together arm in arm. Just a moment in time, but a moment so powerful. I could feel my heart trying to kick its way through my shirt. I knew she was feeling the same. At that very moment nobody else was in our world. I felt reassured.

Every fifteen weeks she would drive up to Bramshill for the 'end of course' black tie dinner. I was always so proud. She would look stunning. Elegant in a ball gown on my dinner suited arm. Quite simply she was my princess and my rock. I was steadied by her support and was able to concentrate, during the weeks and months that followed on the process of providing a stable home for Gavin.

It's true that Gavin gave me some very difficult times over the next three years we spent at Bramshill. Our daily routine was not unlike many families, especially single parents. Breakfast drama! You tell me who 'does want to get up' eat breakfast and get off to school? Gavin had to take medication with food every morning. Every parent/carer in this situation will know and feel the dilemma. I absolutely hated being bossy with him in the mornings, but he simply had to eat and take his tablet. The tablet wasn't a problem, just the breakfast! Surely I couldn't spoil toast.

I'm sure all parents can identify with the constant battle to keep ahead of fussy eaters. Always trying to find new 'fun' stuff for breakfast. Anyway, then off he would go in a taxi to school. It was the same school, so no change to deal with. Then

179

I would don my uniform and toddle off to the training wing and immerse myself in what turned out to be the most professionally rewarding three and a half years of my whole police career.

Over the next two and a half years I was to embark on a phase of this journey for which I had no preparation. Again I have to pay tribute to my sons Lewis and Gavin. They individually showed strength and courage beyond their years. I know Lewis was in a very difficult situation in that he was obstructed in his wishes to have contact with Gavin and I. We exchanged a few precious emails, the odd word on the phone, but it is true to say that we saw very little of each other for nearly three years.

One perfect week's holiday in France was about the sum total contact. It was like having a gaping chasm where half my heart should be. I physically ached for contact with him, but I had made him a promise which I kept; no pressure.

I thought of him many times a day and missed him constantly. I hoped against hope that he would see what I was trying to do. Trying to show someone you love as much as I do him and Gavin that I loved him to the point that I would stay away 'till he was ready. I agonised over my decision in the hope that he was mature enough to really understand the effort I was making was not an excuse for a cop out, or an 'easy life' decision. It was in fact the opposite.

Speaking as a parent, not just a father, our children are our whole reason for living in the majority of circumstances, and I had Gavin's immediate and pressing needs to concentrate on.

Where on earth do I start? I had to get to know him again. I had left the family home in July 1998 and it was now October 2001, over three years of his life had passed and I knew precious little of what had happened for him except the horrific stuff detailed in the social services records.

Surely he must have had some fun, laughed and played with Lewis and friends. I decided that the only way was to ask him. So I went about it with a wholly open and honest agreement with him.

Early on I established that my name was not particularly welcome within his mum's earshot. No surprise there!

That gave me a starting point; first thing was to impress on him that he didn't have to refrain from mentioning his mum to me, in any company or anywhere we may be. She gave birth to him and as such I insisted that he always respect her. Whether he chooses to see her and on what terms as he grows, that also is completely up to him. If he wants to tell me stuff, good or bad, then that's fine. I will not judge, outwardly, nor will I bad-mouth her or any of her family. I'm above that. In turn, if I want to know about anything I wanted to feel free to ask. I promised though not to put him on the spot or test his loyalties. I'd only want to learn about him, from all that I'd missed. It seemed strange to be entering into an agreement with my ten year old son when most kids his age are just expected to do as they are told.

Our circumstances were entirely different, in that for most

of the time there were just the two of us. So we had to develop a way to get the bad stuff exorcised, dwell on the good stuff and really start looking forward to a brighter future, for all.

I suppose this theory was working well until tested practically, for the first time. We were able to talk quite deeply and trustingly.

One evening, Gavin asked could he go and visit his mum for a few hours. My stomach sank, to the point that I was nearly sick. Oh my god, my head was spinning and I knew I had to let him, I'd promised I would never stop him phoning or visiting her. Now it was put up or shut up time. Internally I was in turmoil, externally my answer was a simple,

"Yes of course."

He eventually called and made arrangements to visit the following Sunday. It was only ten miles from the flat so we left early for the drive from Bristol. I simply couldn't eat that morning. Poor Louise, she had to put up all weekend with my pre-occupation and worry again, whilst Gavin was so excited about seeing his mum and Lewis.

Driving along the motorway my mind was spinning because I just felt this wouldn't work, but I knew I simply mustn't let him see my doubts. I had to support him and show him that I meant what I said in our agreement. I was terrified; but honour the agreement I did and even bought a broadsheet Sunday newspaper to read in peace whilst he was at his mum's.

I dropped him off, watched him into the house, all the time desperate for some fleeting glance of Lewis, but to no avail.

About two minutes drive from the house was a car park. I'll wait the agreed few hours there I thought. Hence the real reason for the broadsheet newspaper!

Parked in the very car park I waited desperately many months ago, I sat trying to look engrossed in the paper. I just couldn't settle at first, trying to have faith that he would have a good time and maybe this was the start of a healing process. A process with a long way to go, but a start nevertheless.

The shrill tone of my mobile phone shattered the quiet in the car, it was a number I didn't recognise. It was Gavin's voice from a call box.

"Come and get me please, Mum's being horrible to me."

He'd borrowed twenty pence from Lewis who'd taken him to a call box because he wasn't allowed to call me on the house phone! As I drove the two minutes back to the end of the close, the anger coursed through me like snake venom. If there was one moment when I nearly broke free of my anchor, this was it.

For Christ's sake why? If the visit isn't going well at least let him call from the house, don't leave them to find a call box! I was seething but at the same time immensely proud that the boys had stuck together. Lewis had assumed the role of elder brother and was looking after Gavin. I knew from this moment that the bond between the boys had remained strong, despite their circumstances living apart. A deep positive, being demonstrated out of unbelievably negative behaviour towards them.

Proud as I was of the boys' resilience, it was shrouded by

mounting rage. Determined as I was not to lose my composure if my ex-wife was outside when I returned, I was down to my most basic, and indeed volatile, protective instinct.

Pulling up, Gavin leapt in, still not the merest glance of Lewis that I craved. Deep down I knew Lewis was fine, but I just needed to get Gavin back to the flat. Talk it out, show that Lewis still loved him and had showed he cared. I needed to do all these things.

Yet within minutes of us setting off I was telling Gavin off for calling his mum some really unpleasant things. I was making excuses for her behaviour, again. Why the hell was I protecting her? Maybe I was protecting him, from an irreparable opinion of his mother. We all deal with emotional upset in different ways. This didn't mean she didn't love him but at this moment it was difficult convincing him; I couldn't let him believe the opposite. He has dealt with so much in his few years and no doubt there was more ahead, but at ten years old, please not this. This day ended unsurprisingly with tears from both of us.

A visit was tried once more, and again with similar catastrophic results. How often do I allow him to get hurt like this? How often do I allow Lewis to see this? Every parent will recall the times when the little ones start to walk. Those first few faltering steps: step, step, tumble, cry, step, crunch, cry, step, step, step, step and eventually they are walking. It seems a macabre process letting them fall a few times 'till they sort themselves out. Even as I write this a grin breaks across my face as I remember my boys first few steps. Memorable points indeed. As was this point, but for all the wrong reasons.

I thought long and hard over the next few days. I must let him arrive at his own decisions. This one included. Shielding them from some truths is ok, but this had to be from his own reasoning, and indeed if he had to hurt along the way I would be there to pick up the pieces. He soon realised for himself that he didn't like this and began to make do by calling his mum one evening a week.

These calls I suppose were his way of accepting that for now, visits were out of the question. Again I gave him the privacy he needed and he would take the phone to his bedroom. I would turn up the TV or music so as not to seem intrusive. I couldn't, however, help hearing one repeated question, many times per call. "When can I come and see you again."

Several calls ended with him shouting down the phone, pleading to speak to Lewis. After the calls Gavin would lay on his bed crying, and searching for answers as to why he wasn't getting to see his mum and brother. Like when they tumble, I did my best to pick him up, steady him and offer all the love and support I have in me, hoping that it's enough to make him believe he really is loved. Hoping that in his ten year old reasoning, he can see that I love him twice as much as a normal dad therefore making up, for now, for his pain. I hoped so.

He would regularly fall asleep sobbing. I would sob at the sight of his tears and the feel of his pain. Why can't all kids be shown the love they need, on which to flourish, to grow, to be

185

happy? Love is free.

So often over the years I have heard separated parents saying "I miss them so much, but what can I do, I can't beat the system!"

Correct, you can't beat the system, but you can challenge it. You can make it work for you. Just because you are a mum or dad, a full time working parent, it doesn't mean you have to accept the role of, distant provider. We can challenge the stereotypes and change things for ourselves.

I firmly believe we are all, parents or not, born with a bottomless pit of love inside us. Some choose to release it and live by it; others may choose to suppress it, while others are unfortunate in that the experience or event to release it never arrives. However for most of us, once we become parents, the lid is taken off and the love begins to flow, hopefully towards the children. Uncontrollably at first, and then guided by our experiences and judgment.

Just because a bureaucrat in a government agency, or possibly an ego driven solicitor has an idea of your role, it doesn't mean they are right. Please, please if you feel the love, the deep, all-consuming love and emotion then be guided by it.

Emotion is such a powerful force. In my case it was driving me to achieve things I would have never have achieved had I listened to the powers that be, if I hadn't challenged the system where would I and my sons be now?

One of the stock phrases used by solicitors and barristers is taking instruction. Don't forget, that if you believe you are in the right, you can be strong. Remember, they work for you, they advise you on law, but they do not tell you what is best for you, or your children. Listen to them by all means, but you must stay in control.

~

As Gavin and I settled into the daily and weekly routine of our new life many things began to calm down. We both slowly adjusted to each other again. We went fishing regularly, cycled now and again as well as travelling many miles in my faithful old green Rover. We visited family as often as possible, both sides of the family. Just because his mum and I had separated didn't mean one set of grandparents, aunts, uncles and cousins had to be lost.

Encouraging contact between Gavin and Lewis and the extended family was wonderful for their sense of belonging and self-esteem. Weekend and school holiday periods staying with relatives and playing with cousins, on both sides of the family was nothing more than natural, but had started to decline. So to rebuild this connection, have fun and even get a little spoiled from time to time was paramount in my mind. These short breaks also gave me time to relax and refresh in the knowledge that they were gaining what was rightfully theirs, whilst always knowing that I was there, in the background and only a phone call away, if needed. We were all starting to benefit from a more relaxed life style.

OPENING UP TO MY FEELINGS

Strangely, I never wanted to discuss all my pent up feelings with Louise at the weekends. The weekends were our time, to laugh, go out for dinner or I loved to cook, an absolute passion of mine. Plus the fact that my pre-occupation over the previous three years or so had put such a strain on our relationship it was important for special time just for us without my strains.

Now, as I was entering a different life, I was much happier within myself and although I missed Lewis to a degree that I can't even describe, I had to concentrate on Gavin, at least in the short term. I had my dream to keep chasing, but he needed me in practical terms on a daily basis. I had to make do with the odd e-mail and call when possible to try and reassure Lewis that I was always there for him if he needed, and should he need, then wild horses wouldn't keep me from him.

Again when I least expected it, another person was to enter my life, during tough times, and ultimately have such a profound effect that it was to change me as a person forever. A quiet, unassuming Welsh guy had been posted to the college and walked past the office door, unbeknown to me whilst I was having a brief head-in-hands moment. He didn't know me from the next guy. He could however, see that I was upset but had no idea as to why.

"Hello mate, are you ok. Is there anything I can do?" He asked in a soft Welsh accent.

I looked up at this immaculately groomed and presented guy of about mid-thirties. I desperately wanted to poor my heart out but he didn't want my life story, I assumed.

I made some excuse about a bit of bad news and introduced myself.

He responded in kind. "Hi I'm Paul, Paul Mallet – Gwent."

It was a strange way of introducing ourselves but was normal practice for officers drawn from across the UK and Northern Ireland to staff the regional colleges to add our force to the introduction.

"Ok I'll leave you to it, but if you want a chat give me a shout."

He left me alone, but in those few moments the seed was sown for a deep and lifelong friendship that carried me through the next couple of traumatic and emotion ravaged years.

In common with many blokes, I had suffered from an inability to open up and really talk about my feelings. I think a popular phrase was 'not in touch with the feminine side.' An accusation I think, in hindsight is rightly aimed at many of the 'male gender.'

My life was yet to take so many turns. Paul and I were to have another chance meeting not long after my tearful introduction. One summer evening I was tinkering with my

189

cycle in the garage at Bramshill when Paul pulled up in his new MG soft top sports car and began washing it. Before long we were chatting and I was immediately taken by his warmth. There were many inspirational people here, but he was so warm and 'together' – if you know what I mean!

I began to open up about my reason for crying in the office, he listened and listened, it wasn't exactly a 'man conversation.'

But he was tactile and never once offered a solution. By not offering a 'fix' he was allowing me to open up more fully and indeed shed a tear or two. As I became embarrassed at crying he simply took his opportunity to explain that he, as an openly gay man, living with a regular loving partner had dealt with huge emotional issues too.

He'd originally been married and had a daughter. She was about Gavin's age. Without too much detail he showed me that emotion and love are such a powerful combination and if accepted honestly, they can be the success of any situation. Hide them however, and they will be your undoing. I had found somebody so special who understood me.

On the phone to Louise in the evenings and when home at the weekends it was Paul this and Paul that! I recall her saying, with a soft smile one evening, as I rambled on about Paul,

"You've found the girl friend you need." She was so right.

By such accurate words she was indicating that as the majority of my week was spent at Bramshill, I desperately needed someone there to teach me how to talk about my feelings and to open up. My friendship with Paul developed and my trust in him increased, Paul would regularly call to check how things were. He sat with me through many an evening, especially after Gavin had cried himself to sleep.

I would pick myself up and ring Paul. He knew if I called him at his flat on campus and offered a glass of wine, that I meant I needed an ear and a hug. Never under estimate the healing power of a hug from a true friend. I really had found the 'girl' friend I needed; Paul and I would joke about this many times at Bramshill. I meant it, just as Louise did as a compliment of the highest order. It was testimony to his total warmth and supreme quality as a human being.

We shared many tearful nights, but also more fun times. He was showing me that I had to go out now and again. Many conversations revolved around his daughter and my sons. He showed me that if you loved, truly loved your children and placed them uppermost in your thoughts and actions then they would see and feel this in everyday life, and eventually grow comfortable in the feeling of love and warmth you are delivering.

I didn't need to be in every night so I told myself it was time to go out and have some fun, so we did. Barbeques, cheese and wine evenings, dinner parties. All a bit highbrow but, after all we were in the very fortunate position of having perfect locations for all these events, and more, in the setting of a beautiful country estate.

I wasn't ready to go off campus though, as I was acutely

191

aware that Gavin hadn't long been removed from the child protection register and as such was still high on the local social services radar, and I wasn't prepared to compromise all I had achieved by going off-centre and risk having my level of care brought into question.

Socially, Paul and I became the life and soul of any event we went to. We laughed together – usually outrageously camp, drank together, mostly wine, and occasionally champagne which was his favourite tipple. I want to make clear that I wasn't in any way attempting to belittle Paul or use his sexuality as a way of escaping but I was however using the connection with, and the help of, a quite special person to make those temporary escapes. For that I make no apologies.

Our connection, and the many ways it showed itself prompted a remarkable question one day. Paul and I had been given a class to train together for one course. It was two trainers per class for the fifteen week duration. Suffice to say that there wasn't a dull day in that classroom. Fun, as well as learning, was a given. A disco had been arranged for one evening during the course. We as class trainers really had a duty to attend, officially to support the students' efforts, but we enjoyed it anyway! The freshness and enthusiasm of new officers was a pleasure and the day after this evening of laughs, wine, and a few trips around the dance floor I was approached by a student, with a very worried look.

At my student's request I found a private room and he nervously began to ask,

"We believe one of our trainers is gay, but we can't decide which one!"

Wow, what a compliment to me. Yes, I took that as a huge compliment as I was obviously now being seen in the same light as Paul. A happy, smiling and thoroughly professional individual. It was also a huge compliment to Paul who had helped me come from being a dark, morose individual with no time for fun, to being compared to himself.

My feelings of pride were overtaken by the desire to burst out laughing. I knew instantly that Paul and I would be raising a glass; or two to this question later that evening. However, I had a duty and a responsibility to fulfil first.

So I asked "Why?"

"Just a question on behalf of the class." He replied.

I pressed "From the class, or from You?"

"The class, honestly."

"So do 'the class' or 'you' have an issue with sexuality?"

Now sweating, he responded "No, its just…" his voice trailed.

"Diversity is a huge subject area, and we will cover many sections and topics as we progress through the course. Maybe you could hold on to that question till we reach the appropriate point in the course." I concluded.

After a few awkward mumblings the student admitted it wasn't an issue after all and scampered off. No doubt to remonstrate with those who had asked him to do this. At the end of that course Paul and I were each given a cartoon drawing of ourselves, I think they worked it out!

It was drawn by a very talented student, Troy, and signed by the class. It still has pride of place in my lounge. A wonderful gift indeed with many happy memories.

And so it went, guided and supported by Paul, I became a very open and, I think relaxed individual.

Being so much more relaxed about a majority of things has helped me deal effectively with the really important issues.

Gavin was becoming much more stable, although infinitely capable of wreaking devastation when he saw fit. Not having regular contact with his brother and mum was a constant source of pain to him, but as before he was showing resilience beyond expectation.

He seemingly accepted his situation, but only as temporary. The was a steely determination in him that one day, probably a year or two in the future but never the less, one day, he and Lewis would again enjoy an open and unhindered relationship.

HONOURED

I consider it an absolute privilege to have been in such a trusted and rewarding position within the police force. I remember saying that, whilst Gavin and Lewis were my reason to get up each morning, to work and provide, these folk were my strength. They carried me through some very dark and worrying days, and ultimately got me through. We also had some cracking parties too. It definitely wasn't all work and no play! It always fills me with a warm sense of pride.

Of the many gifts and accolades I received from my students, I think the speech reproduced below says it all; the guy reading this was a six foot plus Hampshire officer called Trevor. It was during the speech phase of the end of the course dinner.

Once the official speeches were over Trevor stood up and begged forgiveness from the gathered dignitaries. He asked me to stand. So I did, feeling very vulnerable but not worried. Trev's class, the infamous '11k' were my class during a particularly tough few months. They had obviously seen me going through tough times, more than I had realised.

He began, "Geoff, it's very difficult to put into words all the good things we can say about you, because there are so

195

many. We have been with you for fifteen weeks. You are one of the funniest, kindest and most caring people I have ever met. You have impacted our lives in such a positive manner. You have shared your knowledge with us in a way that's made it easier to understand. Your teaching methods simply could not be bettered. You have been a pillar of strength to us all, and for that we thank you.

We have laughed with you, and we have cried with you. Saying goodbye is difficult but is made slightly easier in the knowledge that it's not forever. Please don't ever change. It's been special."

As Trevor read these few wonderful words, he was walking towards me through three rows of ball gowned and dinner suited guests, some one hundred and twenty people in all. I was on the top table along with all other instructional staff and guests of honour. Emotionally I was very weak.

I heard his voice crack and waver with emotion, I saw the majority of the people at the dinner reach for their napkins and either openly, or secretly, begin to wipe their eyes. After a few more steps Trev was openly crying. Me too, and shaking so much that I felt a colleague place a firm hand on the back of my left knee and whisper,

"For Christ's sake Geoff please don't fall, hang in there, you deserve these words." Spoken in soft but distinctive Welsh tones I was aware that this hand and voice of support was my dearest, closest friend, Paul.

As Trevor reached the other side of the table to me, he

reached across and pushed the piece of paper into the top pocket of my dinner jacket and opened his arms. I responded and we man hugged over the table. I opened my eyes over his shoulder and looked to the branches of tables expanding away from the top table containing my students. At once they stood up, even partners, here for the first time. The whole room was soon on its feet, deafening applause. It's moments like this when you realise that the very private battle you have been fighting has been noticed by many around you, friends, colleagues and sometimes family who are there in a more subtle way. Not intrusively but keeping an air of normality when and where needed.

Despite a little embarrassment, as I am generally a private person, it felt so lovely to realise that my efforts were being recognised, and people supported me.

I've expanded on this particular incident as these words encapsulated everything I was trying to do. The many other gifts were not for a second, any less valuable to me. I treasure them all. The mini cruise, the countless bottles of wine, the glasses which take a bottle each, the hip flask, the little note book with comments from every member of one class, and the caricature drawing of Paul and myself.

THE KNOCK ON EFFECTS

Louise and I started to argue a lot when I was home. I was becoming very insecure when it came to her, the lady I loved beyond reason. I was as strong as an Ox when it came to courts, social services, solicitors and the like, but so very insecure in relation to the lady who had supported me for so long and indeed from afar.

Try as we did, it was so difficult to find the point when I changed. Was it the tablets? Was it the court battle? Was it settling into a new life as a full time parent? Was it living away? Was Louise beginning to tire of living and working the week without any quality time together other than the weekends, when we tried to cram so much in, there was no time for real rest? Was it simply an accumulation of everything?

So many questions yet very few answers. We would argue then we would find a reason for that particular argument. Unfortunately, the reason for most of the arguments was my insecurity, and a very complicated imbalance in self-esteem.

During the week I was a professional and domestic success. I had achieved my goal albeit Lewis was still with his mum but I knew he was ok. At the weekends the sheer anticipation to go home, as I drove along the motorway, would be interrupted by my worries about what would go wrong. I had the awful downward spiraling feeling that I was eventually to lose Louise.

My stomach would churn and eyes flood with tears at the thought. We always had a dream that in May 2008 when I was to retire from the police service we would go on holiday and at midnight, the day before I was to become a civilian, would raise a glass as time slipped into my retirement day. Our children, four between us would all be over seventeen, and the future would be ours; for us.

In October 2002 we went away for the weekend to Pescara, in the Abruzzo region of Italy. It was a lovely place, on the Adriatic coast. A fashionable resort, popular with the Italians, and although just out of season, was lively enough. Long sandy beaches lined by restaurants of many nationalities. The sea was a lovely warm temperature which occupied me for a couple of hours a day. In the afternoons we would sit in the Piazza in the centre of town, sip wine and watch the world go by. In the evenings the only way to do is get your 'posh togs' on and parade along the fancy shopping areas. When in Italy! It was a break which we both sorely needed, and generally enjoyed but on the final evening we argued and, spent the night locked in our own individual thoughts. Soon after we got home we crumbled again. I really can't recall what caused this but there was something really wrong which neither of us could quite identify. Let alone deal with. Maybe the last one percent of the one hundred needed was missing. No matter how we tried, these derailments became a part of our lives.

In December, Louise booked a cheap seven day holiday to Spain with a close friend for the following May. I felt awful, I never had one moment of mistrust of her in all these years but due to my falling esteem and rising insecurity I simply couldn't cope with the prospect that she may go and meet someone so much better than me, and as I didn't think I was much of a catch any more, that would be it.

Much as I tried to console, and indeed reason with myself, I really couldn't handle it. The saying 'If you love someone – set them free, if they return then they really are yours and if they don't, then they never really were,' rang in my head for the next six months.

Every time she bought something for her holiday I would plunge into silence. Why couldn't WE go away? I really felt that if we could, in our hectic lifestyles, find a spare week off then surely it should be together? Maybe I was being selfish, I don't know. Maybe my insecurity just added to the collateral damage.

We continually argued over this until the departure. It was a midweek night flight from Bristol. I lay in bed at Bramshill picturing her walk out of the house, pulling the red suitcase she had bought for the trip down the garden path and closing the gate behind her.

The tears were rolling down my face again. As I pictured the gate closing I couldn't help feeling I would never see her again. The thought of life without her was too awful to contemplate. Yet when my phone 'buzzed' that night and it was Louise telling me she'd checked in, would I wish her a good trip? I simply couldn't. Not for a second did I wish her any harm, far from it.

But, I couldn't wish her a good and happy holiday. I felt sick. I was ripped apart by insecurity and rightly or wrongly, I just felt I was at a very low point and desperately needed a show of my importance to her. Maybe put it off, not cancel it, just till I am more secure. Potentially more worryingly was that her text could have actually been the show of my importance. But, it felt like a dagger to my heart. I simply couldn't thank her for it by wishing her well.

That coming weekend I took Gavin camping to the New Forest. An area I loved. We went cycling to the Isle of Wight by way of the little ferry from Lymington. We both loved camping.

A week later and it was time to go home for a few days. Gavin was at his aunts because she knew I was going home to see what was left of Louise and I. She and her friend were due to arrive back about 4am. I was duly at Bristol Airport to meet her. Delay after delay meant the plane finally landed three hours late. As she appeared through the arrivals gate she was alone. Her friend, whom I had absolutely no desire to talk to had hung back and would get a taxi. I stood in the terminal shaking, wanting to cry but strangely angry. I drove us home and straight to bed. It had been a long night and tiredness on top of the emotion would not be a good basis for a discussion of such delicacy.

Later that day, after some sleep we tried to be normal, to be ourselves as she told of a week spoiled by rain and more rain, a bus crash and change of airport. I didn't enjoy the fact that she hadn't really had a good time, but there was certainly a feeling of 'serves you right.' To this day I'm not proud of feeling that way but I'm trying to be totally honest about my feelings throughout this entire journey. Stress plays an enormous part in altering our rational thinking. How could I feel so utterly invincible in my professional and parental life, yet wholly worthless in my relationship with Louise?

After that holiday I felt as though I had lost a piece of my heart. The piece that had loved her totally, I still loved her deeply but from here on felt I was always doing the chasing and, therefore, not willing to give my heart and soul to the degree I had done before.

I had no idea why I'd changed towards her, and this didn't sit at all comfortably with me. After all the soul searching, I felt as though I knew myself so well. However, this was now a different set of feelings and emotions. Ones that I had dismissed as I brought my parental feelings and emotions to the fore whilst fighting for the boys. I had to have a long think about how to deal with this before I erupted like a volcano and blew the whole relationship to pieces. I was very worried because I now realised they weren't dismissed feelings and emotions, but merely pushed below the surface. I spoke to Paul many times and eventually took his advice; I needed counselling! Initially I was horrified at the prospect but soon realised that I was no longer under the kind of scrutiny I had been prior to the court hearings, and nothing could be inferred about my suitability any longer. I settled to the idea and further realised that taking this step could only be seen as a positive one, should anyone seek to question my motives.

I contacted my occupational health department who arranged a series of sessions for me, each followed a similar pattern, with me being asked a set of gentle questions, I never felt as though I was being interrogated. At least one of these questions would spark something deep within me, I would then, totally voluntarily, begin to pour my heart out, usually ending in floods of tears and a basket full of soggy tissues, and a little less weight on my shoulders.

Despite being warned about this initial rawness, I was powerless to prevent it, and it had to be allowed to pass in order to dispel the demons within. Eventually it eased and I continued to try to deal with various issues as calmly as possible. It wasn't easy.

The remainder of that year was full of emotional highs and lows of a different sort. The relationship between Louise and I was starting to show the real damage caused by my focus on the issues of the last three years. This damage was buried deep within us and only showed itself when we were either weakened by the fatigue of our busy parenting schedules or under pressure from outside sources. Ordinarily, in these situations our instinct would be to instantly help and support the other without hesitation. Now, however, I felt that we had to make a specific effort to summon the help or support required for each other, and that effort wasn't easy. I don't think we stopped loving or even caring for each other, but we just became more self-protective due to all the blows we had taken in our different ways.

By the spring of 2003 I had become skilled at running the home for Gavin and I, as well as dealing with the various agencies. But Louise and I had spent a few weeks without any form of contact because I'd either gone elsewhere at weekends with Gavin or stayed at Bramshill. I don't recall any specific argument, but sometimes even after the counselling and still learning to understand my emotional self, I would become difficult to live with and the slightest issue could send me silent for weeks. This in turn would pile stress and worry on Louise who was still at our home and trying to maintain some normality.

During this period of silence, which took in a school holiday, Gavin was invited to my sister's in Manchester, so I took the opportunity to book a quick trip to Norway for a few days solitude. Some walking and thinking in the mountains and fjords in an attempt to get my emotional head together.

On my way to the airport I received a solitary text from Louise urging me to take care; which made me realise she did still care and this showed the importance I was so desperate for before. I couldn't stop thinking about what she could mean though and didn't know what to say in my eventual reply.

How wrong was this? The lady I had been through so

much with, and here I was not knowing what to say to her, not even in a simple text. Eventually I simply thanked her for her concern, and promised to send her a card, which I did.

I had a good few days in Norway, made all the better by exchanging a few texts with Louise.

In July, Louise and I had moved on from those few texts to and from Norway. We had sorted our differences and so decided to take a relaxing holiday, somewhere warm and far away. Just a week together, to rediscover ourselves, and by September all the plans were taken care of.

I was so proud of Gavin, and to a degree myself, as he made his way at twelve years old through the maze that is terminal one at Heathrow on a September morning, for his flight to Manchester to spend a week with my sister and nephews. Thus allowing Louise and I to return to Heathrow that same evening for a flight to Oman.

Oman is a wonderful place. Friendly people, very pro-British and the area we stayed in, around the Al Sawadi islands was pure bliss. A week in the sun, a week of peace and rediscovery. Gavin's flight departed on time mid-morning and once he was airborne I set off for the short drive back to Bramshill. I was giddy with excitement that Louise was travelling towards me on the same motorway from Bristol. I arrived home and she was safely at the flat. I finished my packing as typical, pre-holiday nervous chatter filled the air until Paul, who else, arrived to take us to the airport.

As Louise and Paul exchanged greetings hugs I couldn't

help feel that there was a degree of 'thank you' in hers. Paul knew everything of the trauma we had so far survived. Louise knew how much he had helped me, Gavin and indirectly us both. I on the other hand had so much to thank him for already, that every time I looked at him I had 'thank you' in my eyes.

Eventually it was time to return to Heathrow for our own flight. After a very excited forty minute drive we alighted at terminal three in the late afternoon sunshine. Paul gave us both a hug and wished us a good time. Again the softness of his tone disguised the depth and sincerity. I remember thinking to myself that without him, I have absolutely no doubt that we wouldn't have been standing there. Once checked in, and again the security procedures dealt with we both enjoyed a large glass or two of red wine, before we drifted amongst the sparkling array of upmarket shops in terminal three. As I have a liking for smart but understated watches I chose to focus in on the Rolex shop to laughingly see which item I could least afford!

A couple more glasses of wine and very soon we were aboard a huge Gulf Air plane climbing above the London lights. I had never flown at night before so my eyes were wide open taking-in the spectacle of London alight below.

We ate and soon Louise was asleep. I admired her ability to sleep on planes. I on the other hand was far too excited to sleep and continually, stared out of the window, who knows what I was to see at forty thousand feet in total darkness, but I sure wasn't going to miss it. At one point the pilots made an announcement that was really quite bizarre. "We are flying due south with Iran to our left and Iraq to the right." These were two countries I had only seen and heard of in the media for varying reasons, mostly conflict, and here I was high above and between them.

I was sat by a window on the right and so looking down on small pockets of light which were Iraqi towns and villages. I couldn't help pondering: was my present view, similar to that of US & Coalition bomber pilots not too long ago?

Possibly, who knows, but thought provoking at the time? We landed in Bahrain and the plane virtually emptied. Within an hour we were up again and on the final hour long hop to Muscat, Oman. It was now daylight and I passed the hour gazing at the desert which was another first, and after a white knuckle approach through the mountains we landed. A huge distance in miles and culture from the London night we had left behind.

The heat and scenery were both intense as we made our way from Muscat to our resort an hour's drive north along the coast. It is a truly stunning region. I was even grateful that the mini-bus air-conditioning unit was dripping ice cold water on me for the whole journey.

Over the next week I reveled in falling back in love with Louise. Even when respectfully draped in linen and a head scarf she just oozed class. Very soon we were lazing around the pool for days at a time. She was the picture of elegance, and contentment. I was like a hyperactive five year old wanting to be everywhere at the same time, twice!

I slowly relaxed and there was a moment when we were in the pool, alone. I was standing with my head just above the water and Louise floating on her back with her head hooked over my shoulder. A moment so utterly together, words would have been a crude interruption to this most intimate of connections.

A connection so true, we have since discussed how close I was to asking her to marry me, and she admitted she would have accepted without hesitation. We loved and laughed the rest of our holiday.

Alas the holiday came to an end and, after a comfortable flight home we emerged from terminal three at Heathrow. Paul was there with a big smile. I will never forget his words, or my thoughts, at that moment.

"How good do you two look?"

'Not as good as I felt,' were my thoughts.

The next day was bitter sweet, as it was always going to be. Louise returned home to Bristol, and I went back to Heathrow. Gavin boomed through arrivals and my delight at being with him again was just a lovely feeling. We swapped gifts, and stories of deserts and camels and all things exciting. Back to school for Gavin the next day and work for me as the post-holiday reality stick struck a firm blow.

DARK MOODS

I was introduced to my new class, the sharp, dark contrast of my deep suntan against my glowing white shirt was incredible and the topic of much conversation, and indeed envy I expect.

However good I felt I looked on the outside it was vastly superseded by my feelings of joy and well-being on the inside. Louise and I were in love again, I was feeling recharged and Gavin was coping well with our new life, he was displaying great strength of character. He knew I was there for him, always. This feeling of all round happiness was a feeling I thought had long deserted me. Louise and I were even beginning to talk about my retirement trip, a mere five years away. Emotionally, I was glowing.

In the New Year we repeated the 'let's have some time away' thing. This time just a long weekend. Gavin excitedly off to Manchester via Heathrow again, and Louise and I to Palermo, Sicily. Palermo turned out to be fabulous place, and warm enough to wear a t-shirt in January. It was a place full of mafia intrigue and of course plenty Vino Rossi. Not quite the same tan on our return, but very much the same feelings of warmth, contentment and feelings of being able to love and be loved.

These feelings of contentment were to be tested again as a bombshell was dropped at work. The initial training wing were called together and informed that our contracts at Bramshill were over by June.

Oh my God, how will Gavin deal with moving permanently to Bristol?

He loved Louise but could he live full time with her and vice versa? How would she and her two react to us back home full time? How would Louise react to the increased scrutiny of social services who were bound to show up when we moved home permanently? Even though he was no longer on the child protection register, we would never realistically be free of the social services for a couple of years yet. I totally understood the intrusion of the unannounced visits, annoying as they were but in truth they would lessen as time went by and we settled at home.

Questions racked through my mind over the coming months as to how we were going to cope. We'd already booked separate summer holidays, Louise was having quality time with her two to Lake Garda while Gavin, my nephew Sean and I to Sardinia. It worked really well spending time with our own children as well as together too, none of them were missing out.

Louise and I were keen on having our own late season holiday as we did last year to look forward to after the school holiday period.

Our idyll had been thrown into turmoil again but we can deal with this, I'm sure, I thought. After all we have dealt with in the past five years, this was just realignment.

The summer break up of the schools heralded a chaotic few weeks for us. Louise and her two were loading the car for their short trip to Bristol Airport as Gavin and I arrived to see them off on a bright Saturday morning. Bright July sunshine, and the air of excitement tangible. Gavin and I followed them but went to the far side of the airport as they went to the long term parking area.

Eventually we saw them board their plane and take off into a clear blue sky. Something was wrong. Was Louise just preoccupied with the holiday, the flight and the thought of collecting the hire car and driving across Italy, or was our imminent permanent return getting to her in some way?

My relationship with her son had always been difficult but as it was only weekend based, we developed coping strategies that worked most of the time. Now it was to be full time, so I wondered if this was this on her mind? Foolish to think otherwise; as it was certainly on mine!

We weren't to depart for Sardinia until the Monday, nine days later. I had the small matter of a London to Paris charity cycle ride to attend from Wednesday to Sunday. The arrangements were a logistical masterpiece and all the plans worked liked clockwork, but deep in my mind was the niggling feeling that something was wrong, or at least not quite right between Louise and me.

After four days of cycling and thinking, along with Phil and many others I arrived in Paris to a fanfare under the Eiffel

Tower, and a huge crowd of families meeting their various loved ones. I was crowded and welcomed, yet strangely alone. So many riders had friends or loved ones there to meet them. I knew that Louise simply couldn't be there – she was on her way home from Italy, but I felt there was a gap developing between us again and it bothered me deeply.

After all this, please, please don't let me lose the happiness I was again starting to enjoy. I grabbed a bottle of the free champagne from the finish area and rode off to the hotel slugging the contents as I rode the few hundred yards alongside the Seine. Once at the hotel my bike was taken and stored for the trip back to UK and my bag and room key handed to me. I was again roomed with my dear friend Phil.

I was elated at my performance on my bike over the last four days but now I was somewhat preoccupied. After the holiday to Sardinia with Gavin and Sean it was to be home for good.

Phil arrived long after my bottle was empty and sadly, as he was teetotal, he didn't bring any with him! As we chatted and prepared for the prize-giving and gala dinner that evening I just wanted to be at home.

The next morning I was away early. My bike transported to London where Phil would collect and store it till I returned. I boarded the Metro heading for Charles de Gaul airport with only a small holdall and a mild hangover.

It was lovely to meet Gavin and Peter at Heathrow. Soon we were back at the flat, packing the last bits for Sardinia and preparing to leave the flat and the Bramshill estate for the last time. It was to be the end of one era as well as the start of another.

We met Sean at Heathrow the following morning and I was looking forward to all of us relaxing and having fun.

Sardinia was a pure delight, clear blue sea, safe, clean, almost white beaches and very, very warm. We all had a fabulous time and included a ferry trip to Corsica for the day. It was so good to see Gavin having a good time after the last few years. As I watched him looking so happy for the entire week, I knew I'd done the right thing.

Sadly Lewis wasn't there and tried to console myself. Still, a tear or two appeared one warm evening as I sat outside the tent with a glass of red and dwelt longer on what I couldn't achieve in that he wasn't with us, instead of enjoying what I had achieved. Eventually I pulled myself together by focusing on all the positives.

The counselling was now paying dividends, quite a while after but never the less it was beginning to help. I was able to turn my thought processes around from negative to positive very swiftly and based on real things I'd achieved. I hadn't been trained to transport myself into some false utopia as a quick temporary fix. I knew I had done well and knew how to use that knowledge. When I watch sportsmen or women being interviewed on television they always start by saying how well they played, then maybe a few words on things that weren't so good and what they would do to remedy it, then finish on a positive point and look forward to their next game. This process worked really well for me too. So, I sat and let the late evening sun bake away any further worries.

The plan, as we landed at Stansted was to drive to my sister's in Manchester to take Sean home and stay a day or two, before making the final journey home to coincide with Louise arriving home.

The reality was slightly different though, a long day travelling after a hot and sticky start in Sardinia. My mind would wander with thoughts of seeing Louise again in just a few days. We'd been apart for approximately two weeks and my stomach would knot with anticipation at the thought of holding her again, and seeing her smile.

The following morning, a change of plan. Gavin wanted to stay with my sister and come home in a week or so, which fitted in well while Louise and I went on the mini-cruise. So I shot off home full of anticipation.

Three hours later, as I walked up the garden path, the kitchen door opened and there she was. Resplendent, and with a very familiar and warming smile breaking across her face. We sat outside, had a couple of glasses of wine and discussed our recent travels. Here we were, sat together at home doing what we were so very good at, sipping and chatting. Quaffing wine in a civilised manner and putting the world right.

Indeed our world felt like it was finally coming together.

IS IT REALLY OVER?

Louise and I headed for Portsmouth and the cruise. It was wonderful having her to myself again. The ship was huge, although a car ferry, and a very big one at that, it was beautifully fitted out to satisfy the passengers for a journey of over thirty hours. After settling in on board we enjoyed a lovely dinner as the ship sailed out of port on a beautiful evening.

However, the whole trip was a catalogue of disasters. Wrong cabin, rude bar staff, and whilst we made the best of it, it was clear something was amiss between us. I was certainly very touchy when I felt she said the wrong thing. Most of the time for no real reason at all. Maybe I just needed to learn to be with her again after all we had been through. There would undoubtedly be some wounds to heal and scars to tolerate.

The real plus point was watching the whales and dolphins as we sailed sedately, in the warm sun, across the flat calm Bay of Biscay, and return over the three days. The sight of these massive yet sociable creatures was incredible. A sight that will stay with me for all time.

As we docked back in Portsmouth we were high on the observation deck looking down on the manoeuvres as this huge ship was 'parked' with consummate ease. I was in awe of the skill of the people mooring the vessel.

As I held Louise in my arms for the final moments of the trip I was also beginning to worry about what was to greet us at home once we all got back together. I could feel the tension building in my mind. Louise is as passionate and a protective mother, as I am a father and I'm convinced that these instincts were the bedrock of her ability to understand and support my efforts towards the boys.

Inevitably I suppose once we all settled into life together, the squabbles began. Small at first and usually between the kids, but would then rise to arguments between us. There is no place in this book, or my heart for blame.

Arguing was and still is something I hate. I feel that if you get to the point where emotion has taken over from reason, as is the case with most domestic arguments then the opportunity to resolve a situation is lost. Emotion is the fuel and is always needed but mustn't be allowed to take over driving.

We were two fiercely protective parents when the kids became involved and would each rally to the defence of our own whenever allegations were being thrown around. We would throw protective barriers around them, and in doing so put barriers between ourselves.

I could see that it wasn't doing Louise any good either. Her beautiful smile absent more than present, instead her face contorted with anger and anguish. My heart was breaking slowly and, I'm sure hers was too.

After all we had been through individually and collectively it wasn't supposed to be like this.

Louise arrived home after collecting her son from football training while I was fitting the shower screen. Without a word from me she came straight up to the bathroom, and perched nervously on the edge of the toilet seat. I sat on the edge of the bath and aimlessly fiddled with the screen.

My mind had been racing but was very calm now. She didn't seem surprised when I said I was no longer prepared to put up with the situation between us. Whether it was the collateral damage of the previous five years, our individual lives which we had developed whilst I had been working away or our time had just run its course, the clear fact was that we were tearing each other apart.

I couldn't and indeed wouldn't ask her to choose between her children and me. Not in a million years would I, let anyone come between me and mine, so I wouldn't put her in that predicament.

"It's over. We're finished," the words echoed around the bathroom as I spoke.

There were no tears.

"Can I have a hug," she said.

I couldn't even do that now, I felt as if a hug would be hollow, emotionally, I was hollow inside. She didn't deserve that, better no hug than a hollow, meaningless gesture. She walked out of the bathroom. That was it, now all I could hear was silence.

Later that evening we talked, quite calmly. She asked me was she under pressure to move out quickly.

"Of course not," was my instinctive reply.

I can't help drawing the parallel with the custody hearing. The ground work; or damage in this case, had been done in the months before this moment, leaving the final words to be spoken in a few clear but somber moments. Words which reduced all my hopes of spending the rest of my life with this beautiful, warm, passionate and loving lady, to ruins.

I was already missing her and it would only get worse, that was for sure, but hopefully better for us all in the long run.

We tried over the next couple of months to get on with life as best we could. We would try to spend alternative weekends away to give the other space and relaxed time with the kids. We had all the clinical, but heartbreaking discussions. Even pledging to discuss what furniture each would take when the time came for her to move out.

Louise moving out felt like a horrendous prospect. At her request I promised to go away for the weekend when the time came. I was lost again emotionally.

I tried instinctively to protect Gavin from as much of my anguish as I could. He didn't need to see me falling apart emotionally. He was coming to terms with a new permanent home, new school, and new mates.

We spent most weekends at my sisters in Manchester. One weekend following a couple of glasses of red, I agreed that as both my birthday and my eldest nephew Karle's was soon approaching we would go away for a weekend.

I also needed a break, I was desperately missing Louise and I was really struggling to hold myself together.

Karle and I decided on our weekend away, well, Karle did. I had a few glasses of red wine and became Uncle Generous! A title that would plague me for many years.

"Anywhere you want buddy" was my possibly foolish line. He disappeared upstairs to think a while before reappearing and sitting on the arm of my chair.

"New York," he proclaimed. I nearly spat my wine across the room. My sister looked directly at me and said,

"You said anywhere," and so it was.

After the initial shock I was so excited and got to work planning our trip.

A few hectic weeks later we left Manchester airport for the big apple. As Karle and I prepared to go through security, I noticed Gavin was looking tearful. I hugged him and reassured him; I would be back in four days.

"I know," he sobbed, "But I just don't want you to go, you haven't been this far from me before."

The truth was I was feeling exactly the same, but for differing reasons. I had no doubts or worries about his safety at my sisters. I knew exactly where he was. For him though, it was very different. He had no idea of where I would be. No mental picture. I was disappearing into the sky.

This goodbye, albeit only for four days was very painful indeed, as he whispered, "Have a good time."

I felt the coldness of his tears on my face. Peering over his shoulder, I looked at my sister who had a strained expression. She was clearly holding back her tears. Then she blurred; I hadn't managed to hold mine.

Gavin and I had become so utterly combined. We were each other, we understood and we even felt for each other.

It was hard as I turned and went through security and into departures.

"You Ok Uncle Geoff?" asked Karle reassuringly as we sat in the bar.

"Yes buddy, I'm fine ta, it's just upsetting, and we only have each other most of the time."

"You've got us too," said Karle. He really did understand.

"Cheers" as I raised my glass to him.

I realised on our four day trip just how ready I was for a break. What a fabulous time in such a wonderful place, and in such fabulous company. Karle had just turned fifteen and was real good company. We did the lot and walked everywhere.

Four days later, it was a mixture of jet lag and fatigue that arrived back home. Eager to see Gavin, I just needed to be with him again, possibly more for my reasons than his.

Fully recovered from the jet lag, we set off for the drive home. I was a little anxious about seeing Louise again, but eager to see her all the same. I couldn't help caring. I knew there would be no open arms or hugs, that wasn't the way anymore, just polite conversation would suffice.

I opened the back gate and my world collapsed. The

curtain less windows; a path trodden from the patio doors across the back lawn to where I was standing, she had gone, she'd moved out.

My hand trembled as I fumbled the key into the back door and let myself in. She left a note on the kitchen side explaining why that weekend, and I fully understood.

REBUILDING OUR LIVES

The beginning of life without Louise was more horrific than I could have ever imagined. As I checked the half emptied cupboards in the kitchen Gavin ran around the house as if searching for confirmation. The poor kid was devastated again, he had grown to love Louise over the years. She clearly wasn't his mum, and in fairness to her she never tried to be. She was however the lady that loved his dad, the lady with whom he was able to secretly plot the odd birthday or father's day surprise, the lady whom he knew his dad loved so very, very much was now gone.

I knelt on the kitchen floor hugging him as he stood in front of me. I was ripped apart. The dagger in my heart at her final departure had left a wound so deep. This wound however would have to wait to be healed. Gavin was hurting bad and I needed to stop that first. As we knelt and stood in the kitchen there was a tap on the back door.

There stood a neighbour, obviously feeling very awkward having seen Louise move out and not really knowing how I would be feeling. He made a simple, but massive gesture as he offered us the loan of crockery and cutlery until we were sorted.

Gavin, realising that there was very little cutlery left, then proceeded to show me just what a wonderful individual he was. If my fight, love and determination to guide him was ever to be rewarded, this was it. It was a dark drizzly November afternoon, he simply got on his bike, rode to the supermarket and returned with a pack of four sets of plastic knives, forks and spoons. He put them in the drawer in the kitchen proclaiming,

"They'll do for now."

I looked at this thirteen year old boy who was hurting on two fronts, firstly at Louise's departure and secondly at the very visible pain his father was enduring. At this moment, I wished my dad could have seen Gavin, having already fought so much, and dealt with so much heartache yet he had the strength to do that. In that single gesture he inspired me.

"Right that's it," I had to do something, fast.

Something positive, something he could see. Onto the motorbike, both of us and out to the shops before the bank closes. I had been a good customer with regular decent wages and an all-round good account rating, or so I was told at the yearly financial health checks. Now it was time for the bank to help me, to help us. After a mere twenty minutes in the bank we re-appeared, a healthy five thousand pounds better off. A loan of this size was trifling by bank standards and with the minimum of fuss it was put straight into my account.

Now, a continual source of humour within the family is my frugalness. I'm not mean but I refuse to be ripped-off. So, to go on a spending spree so apparently wild, was something that Gavin had never seen me do, but in this case needs must, and all that.

I remember his face as I said things like:

"Do you like that bed?"

"Yes" he'd reply.

"Ok, I'll collect it in half an hour" was my instruction to the member of staff.

"What colour bedding?" I'd ask him.

"Blue"

"Wrap it up,"

Curtains, same routine. I was now on a mission to give Gavin his own space. A sense of ownership of his room, his chosen bed – a high sleeper with desk and futon below with his chosen bedding and curtains, the lot. All bought within an hour and taken home the same evening. I simply had to give him a positive end to the day.

Fortunately the shops were open quite late as it was the start of Christmas shopping hours. Gavin was physically able to help me assemble his bed, but we had a struggle. Picture it if you will; a small box room (he could have chosen the second bedroom but he wanted the smallest one, a bit more of a 'den' I suppose.) After a frantic shopping spree I decided to try and get his bed up, made with his own bedding and curtains that very evening. Bedding and curtains would be easy. The bed however was an epic struggle, added to by his wish to have it in a certain way that required me to saw two pieces of skirting board away to fit it in. I eventually, and in triumph slid the 'shark cage' look-alike bed into place. I think snug would be a good description of its fit.

I stood back, tired, sweating profusely but pleased that I could now put the curtains onto the rail while he made his bed.

"Daaaaad" he said falteringly, in a manner every parent knows is going to be followed by an embarrassing or very difficult question.

"I think I prefer it over there," pointing to the wall under the window - exactly where we had started!

"Ok, let's move it then." I replied in a whisper, again parents will know exactly how I mean. It's a tone that implies, I can't actually look at you, or I'll kill you.

Ten minutes later it was done and with him busily making his bed, I sorted the curtains and stashed my tools. I had been so busy I'd pushed aside the fact that Louise had gone. Until, that was, I went downstairs to make a cup of tea. I was descending into an echoing, sparsely furnished area dotted with reminders. Painful reminders. No curtains, bare walls. Although she had only taken half, it was empty without her.

Our beautiful home that I had sweated buckets getting right, had somehow been violated but not out of malice. Instead perversely, by love.

I filled the kettle, opened the drawer for a spoon and gazed directly at the plastic cutlery which was the final straw. I stooped helplessly over the worktop and cried, at last, for myself. I was lost again. More importantly, where was Louise? Was she alright? I needed to cry for myself, even though it was me that ended our relationship, it didn't mean I wasn't hurting, in fact I was, so very deeply.

I finally reached the lowest point, I was at survival stage. I knew Gavin was busying himself in the excitement of his room and fitting it out as he wished. I could hear him pottering around. He had never been a quiet thing!

I was now on my ass emotionally. I did however have two boys dependant on me to get myself sorted. One was a hundred miles away but never closer emotionally, and the other was upstairs thumping around like a herd of elephants. I also had a secret weapon – myself.

The previous years battles had taught me so much about myself and I knew that painful as this was, I could and would deal with it. If it doesn't kill you, it makes you stronger. As well as relying on my anchor, I can also be a stubborn, determined and single minded individual.

I went and sat in the car and called Paul. I blubbered; he listened, then quietly told me to get on with it, do as I felt right and he would call me the following evening.

~

Whilst studying during my time at Bramshill I was assigned some reading of the works of a philosopher called Rousseau. One area I was particularly taken by was the subject of passive watching. Instead of trying to impress on children, adolescents or indeed adults, your values and demanding or expecting them to adopt them, it was a suggestion, it may be better ultimately to demonstrate your values clearly by your own behaviour in the hope that the child sees you succeed in your daily endeavours. The outcome hopefully being that they adopt some or all of your values as their own, because they have seen them work.

So, I decided to get up cheerful every morning. Deal with work properly because that's what pays the bills, buys food, car and holidays etc. I didn't want to be seen by either of my boys, or anyone else as giving up.

Yes, I would have horribly sad moments. Moments like not being able to say "Goodnight sweetheart" as I turned off the bedside light. I would talk to Gavin about his sad moments and allow him the space to let him unload. My private and sad moments however were not for Gavin, or Lewis to be burdened with at their tender ages.

There would be incredibly funny moments too. Like going out to the shops on the motorbike for just a few bits, and realising it was 'buy one get one free' at the curtain and bedding shop. I was in my element. I love shopping at the best of times but elbow to elbow in a bargain hunt with a bunch of middle aged ladies who clearly felt that a male had no place matching bedding and curtains, was just what I needed. Bring it on! I eventually emerged into the cold evening with several sets of curtains and bedding. I had shopping bags everywhere and oh yes my crash helmet! How on earth would I get this lot home on the bike?

My time in the Royal Military Police motorcycle training wing, and more latterly, a police driving school, was not to be wasted. In training, not to be tried at home, I've ridden standing on the foot rests, standing on the seat or fuel tank, sitting on the handlebars with feet on the front mudguard, even sitting on the seat if feeling conventional and at speeds so high I wasn't able to realise how terrified I really was until I'd slowed down.

So this was, after due thought, a fairly simple matter of sitting on the bike and stacking and stashing it where it would fit. I called Gavin to be waiting outside the garage to help me.

Once I'd piled it all up and was sure everything was secure on the bike, I switched on the lights and kicked it into gear. Here was me thinking this was extreme motorcycling when after all I wasn't breaking any laws. I laughed to myself recalling a family of four, a dog and the week's shopping all on a moped at once on a holiday abroad!

For the next ten minutes I treated my particular area of South Gloucestershire to a display of motorcycling, the like of which they had never seen. My route had consisted of about three miles, one t-junction, three roundabouts then a left, right, left manoeuvre to the back of our house.

Gliding majestically around the roundabouts, timing the entry to them, without stopping, was a bit fraught but I accepted all the admiring beeps en-route.

As I neared our garage Gavin was looking in horror as well as laughing wildly. I stopped, put my foot down and even in such a moment I was able to tilt the bike to the right so it all fell towards the garage. Mission accomplished!

Rebuilding our lives was gathering pace with sad

moment's yes, but also good ones to share. That Christmas Gavin and I went to my sisters. It's true I didn't quite feel strong enough to face a Christmas without Louise. This Christmas was in fact a milestone for me, and for us. I had refitted the house, curtains, bedding, new sofa, even a dishwasher! New cutlery, crockery, 'posh' as well as everyday stuff. Pictures on the walls, table lamps, the list goes on, but we had reinvented the house with our own character.

As I drove north I recall feeling optimistic, I was going back to the place I grew up, Hadfield, on the outskirts of Manchester. It was the first time since Louise had left that we had gone away and therefore the first time I had left without at least saying a polite farewell. I left it empty; it would stay empty and would be empty when we returned. I accepted that it was over and was more relaxed as a result. Who can guess the future, but I was determined to have one. I would grieve for our relationship, but I wouldn't stay in the past.

Near my sister's is an area called Coombs Rocks. A huge expanse of open crescent shaped rocks and hills giving fantastic sweeping views over the famous Kinder Scout in one direction, and the distant outline of the congested city of Manchester the other way. I spent many a happy summer camping and staying up there as a kid, and many a walk up over the coming years when visiting.

On one such walk I emerged on the east face of the hill, just to take in the moment I found a big boulder on which to sit and contemplate life. It offered fantastic views over Chunal, and other peak district villages.

I adopted this rock. It was where I could sit and talk to myself, think quietly, talk with dad and even watch and wonder at the low flying airliners en route into or out of nearby Manchester airport. Where had this plane come from or where was it going? It became a place of private contemplation, but not just when times were tough and I needed breathing space. But, when all was well in my world too, I would often wander up there, take stock of all I'd achieved, and smile to myself.

Christmas and New Year came and went and whilst they all tend to blur into one over the years, I do remember this one being a peaceful and relaxing one. I recall standing looking out of the lounge window towards the rocks, and my boulder at midnight on New Year's Eve and feeling positive about the years to come.

However, it was soon time to head for home and I would be lying if I didn't admit to some anxiety as we got nearer and eventually arrived. I knew all would be ok, but just flashbacks I suppose. I'm convinced that Gavin was aware of my tension.

I was still concerned about Louise and missed her. As we entered, first the back garden then the kitchen, all was well. I allowed myself a moment's self-satisfaction, before unpacking.

This year was to be a year of getting used to our new lifestyle. Indeed without the Home Office bonus for working away, on my wages alone and without Louise's income things were definitely going to be different. Holidays would be camping, which wasn't a problem because we both loved the outdoors. I was however determined to make Gavin's birthday in March, his fourteenth, a birthday to remember and I knew exactly what to do, I had a plan.

After spending a few secret evenings on the computer I called him into the spare room where I had the screen covered up and asked him to press enter on the keyboard. He looked at me a little oddly for a while but eventually, knowing I wouldn't do anything bad, he pressed it.

"Ok, now look at the screen" I said.

His eyes widened, filled with tears before he flung his arms around me. The lines on the screen displayed words to the effect that, your trip to New York has been successfully authorised! He totally deserved no less after what he had endured in his short life.

Our combined wish to make this trip utterly perfect was for Lewis to be with us but sadly that couldn't be. I had to hold firm and explain as best I could to Gavin that to pressure Lewis, even for a trip as good as this, would ultimately upset him.

Our lives were beginning to slowly get on track and I was starting to accept life without Louise. I went on over the next couple of years to have a couple of relationships, but I simply wasn't ready. Not fully over her, but not bitter either.

I was becoming best at being a 'mummy-daddy.' Probably not the most macho of nick-names, but one I am immensely proud of. I feel really good though that I was able to give sufficient extra to be awarded mummy-daddy status by Gavin.

DEVELOPING BONDS

As you know I've had help and advice along this journey from several inspirational people, but there is one person however, ordinary, to the point of being extra ordinary in his own unassuming ways who came into our lives and made an enormous difference.

During my time at Bramshill when things were tough Social Services offered respite care for Gavin. An arrangement where Gavin would go to a registered and trained carer for a weekend every six to eight weeks thus allowing me time to just relax, spend time with Louise as it was then, or give us time to go away somewhere. I took the opportunity to do all of these several times.

In looking for a suitable carer family to place Gavin with, the Social Services aim was to, as close as possible replicate the home situation. Here was the problem; finding a family consisting of one bloke, who was trained and suitable. There weren't many but they assured me they were trying. Trying to find a carer who was male, lived alone, ran his own home and was active enough to do days out and had common interests with Gavin; mainly cars. He had to live fairly close, within Hampshire. He also had to have experience of boys of Gavin's age, with ADHD and the problems there would undoubtedly be. He also had to be sufficiently confident to deal with the controlled drug medication Gavin was on at the time. As you can imagine, there was literally thousands of suitable candidates – not.

There was however, one, Peter, it's a shame he is only a 'Mr.' This guy should be knighted. Folk like Peter should be where the country looks for its real heroes. Social Services insisted on bringing Peter to our flat to meet me and see our situation. If we were Ok with each other, stay on and meet Gavin when he came home from school. As parents, we go with instinct a great deal and I immediately felt at ease with Peter, and I knew Gavin would too. He was a kind, caring chap, but as Gavin found out a time or two, no pushover.

Gavin spent many happy weekends with Peter. So much so that when he ceased doing the respite care, he had become such a good friend that Gavin still went to spend time with him. So it was only right and fitting that Peter was our first 'staying' guest at our home in Bristol.

It was no surprise to me when Gavin realised that it was school holidays prior to the weekend that Gavin and I were to be in New York, he asked to spend the few days with Peter. In fact only meeting me en-route to the airport. Peter even put some dollars in his birthday card as we were in fact to travel on his fourteenth birthday.

So Gavin was away at Peter's waiting for his trip to New York. I on the other hand was working, packing, checking tickets, money etc. following all the normal parenting stuff. All the things that made my daily routine, and I wouldn't have swapped it for the world.

Terminal Three at Heathrow is an eclectic mix of long haul travelers, which isn't filled with cheap airlines as is demonstrated by the array of designer luggage, stacking out the flotilla of trolleys being rumbled around by well-heeled travelers. It is straight away clear that this terminal doesn't, as a rule, deal with your short hotel weekend away, one holdall or rucksack traveler. Yet, given the class of traveler it does cater for, it was really austere, dimly lit and not at all welcoming. It was all steel and aluminium, purely designed for swift efficiency, a bit like the steel and aluminium of a chip shop!

Whilst checking in for the flight I handed over our passports with a note included pointing out that it was Gavin's birthday, that this was his special treat and asked if we could have a window seat for us to fight over please, if not an upgrade! I also asked in my note for her not to mention it.

With a few sideways comments it was communicated to me that we had been given two really good extra legroom seats and put on the upgrade list if there were spaces left when boarding. Grateful for at least a better economy seat we went through security and into the shopping area.

Then came a moment of realisation for me in that although it was to be an adventure for Gavin, it was about travelling to other countries to experience lifestyle and possible culture differences for him too. People often see travel in a different light. An assistant in the book/magazine outlet asked Gavin cheerfully where he was going and when he replied,

"New York."

This young lady rocked us both by saying, "Wow, just think of all the trainers you can buy."

She obviously had a different outlook to travel. In a strange sort of way it reminded me not to make the trip too much of a lesson. Try to let him take the lead a bit too, or at least his wishes.

Once on board we indeed sat in two lovely leg friendly seats, no-one in front, just a partition and by a window, perfect. Just as we are settling this lady and her daughter said we were in their seats. A fearsome lady and brandishing two boarding cards which she was clearly not afraid to use! As I began to protest with a similar display of paper weaponry it was clear that blood would be spilt, until a stewardess was swiftly between us like a boxing referee. She took all four boarding cards and vanished towards the front of the plane, leaving us in a stand-off.

The stewardess returned, looked directly at Gavin and said "You're through here sweetie," in a soft American drawl, "You too Pop."

We followed her into the Business Class section.

I simply couldn't resist a look back and smile at the lady as she and her daughter settled into our old seats before the curtain was whooshed across the aisle, and removing us from the envious eyes of the masses. I kind of felt sorry for the daughter, having to spend the next eight hours next to that simmering volcano. When I say I felt sorry for her, my feelings lasted about twenty seconds, just long enough for my bum to hit the huge blue leather super reclining seat and a bowl of warmed cashew nuts appear on my table.

The arrival of the nuts was followed by a pure vision of beauty gliding towards me uttering the words,

"Champagne Sir"?

Fairly confident it was free I replied; "Yes, I think so, thank you."

We hadn't even pushed back, but I manfully managed to get this and one more glass down my face before taxiing to our holding position at the end of the runway. I was grateful we were in a wide bodied Boeing Triple Seven, otherwise my huge, smug smile which was so wide, would have been responsible for untold damage to both sides of this posh class cabin.

The flight was smooth, and as sophisticated as I have ever travelled. Fine food served on real plates, linen napkins to catch my working class dribbles and a highly acceptable 'Shiraz' served in a real wine glass, and regularly topped up. Gavin was almost lost in the seat next to me but I assumed he was there somewhere due to the constant stream of food delivered to that area.

I think the stewardess took a shine to him. As we winged our way over the Atlantic my thoughts drifted to the selection of people who, over the previous few years, tried all they could to bring me down, and hoped thus to stop me getting custody. I had succeeded thus far and Gavin was in good, albeit slightly pissed hands at this exact moment! Naturally I thought of Lewis. Yes it would have been wonderful for him to be with us. It just wasn't possible this time, but one day buddy, one day.

I had learnt also not to dwell on what I couldn't do at any given moment. Save it for the future and concentrate on what I can do now; so I did. I raised my glass which was swiftly topped up, pressed a button to release the footrest from my seat and smiled!

The few days in New York with Gavin were a blast, even being detained by NYPD as a terrorist! Gavin got me to ask the NYPD to show him around a police station and car. They were really cool, and he loved it. He even sat in the front of a vehicle with a cop, I in an ironic change was relegated to the back seat. At Gavin's request the cop ran my details through the computer. How much 'not fun' was it when my details came back as an alias of somebody wanted in connection with terrorist activities! The rear doors automatically locked, I was isolated in the back, police units racing to this cop's aide and me definitely not free to leave. It was a sweaty ten minutes until he satisfied the dispatch system that I really was just a normal British guy, and a cop to boot.

It also got a bit 'unfunny' as I walked in and out of various shops in Manhattan with Gavin wandering behind, using his hands as a megaphone to announce,

"The terrorist has left the building!"

New York was still very twitchy and I had to impress on him that what he thought of as just poking fun at dad, millions of Americans might not!

Our trip to New York led to Gavin and I being able to joke around a little. On the final day we had several hours to carry on the adventure, we wandered the streets as we waited for our night flight when we saw a cable car heading over the river to Roosevelt Island which intrigued us greatly. A return ticket was very inexpensive, so we were soon aboard. From high up we could see a baseball park on the island. In truth there wasn't much on the island but we managed to have a great time playing a game of baseball with an imaginary bat and ball. It had been exactly the trip I wanted for his birthday.

I had a sense that things were going generally well for us both now. We arrived home to the news that the local education authority had realised that Gavin, although having a few problems at school due to his ADHD, was intelligent enough to go straight to a college environment. In mainstream school he didn't work well with others whom he felt were less able. This invariably led to conflict, outburst and several exclusions. The college placement offered, while still covering key skill areas such as Mathematics, English Language and basic sciences also introduced the students to more skill based subjects, and in Gavin's case it was the building trade. He loved it, and whilst not entirely trouble free he responded well to the more mature approach.

September marked a point when I took a great deal of

personal satisfaction. Lewis would finish school at the end of the coming educational year the following July. I had a letter from the Child Support Agency announcing that my liability would end when he actually left school, unless he went into further education, Lewis was already clear that he wasn't intending to go to college or university. I wouldn't lie by saying the extra money wasn't going to be a great help. Moreover, it was another moment when I could stand tall and say that I had paid, willingly, every penny required.

I can honestly face my boys and say I did all I could for them.

A SILVER LINING

As the boys' mum and I were now bringing up one son each I applied to the CSA for a re calculation of my payment to her. I had hoped that as we each had one son the Child Support Agency would be out of the equation.

I was really disappointed when they ruled against me on the basis that her working hours were insufficient to asses her for a maintenance payment to me and I had to continue with my payments as normal, I just couldn't believe it. I felt the system was discriminating against me in that it allowed such a manoeuvre. I just sat in the dark and cried. I was devastated. I still had to pay a large amount to her for Lewis which I didn't begrudge one bit. But she wasn't required to contribute for Gavin, how can that be right? Lewis was my son and I had responsibilities which I intended to meet in full, both financially and emotionally where possible, regardless of the cost. However this decision was yet another knock and just didn't seem fair.

The boys were my anchor and added to the anchor I now had a dream. I began to dream of a moment in which one day both boys and I would be linked, arms around shoulders, as three happy and smiling blokes. This wasn't a sleepy dream, but a passing day dream to enjoy many times if a suitable break in the busy days and evenings allowed.

I didn't know where or when this picture or moment would happen, but I knew it would.

Obviously the Child Support Agency decision made life financially tough but I just had to get on with it. Private as I am, I felt supported enough in the confines of our office to share my frustrations with close colleagues. We all need to vent our feelings within a safe environment from time to time.

Cometh the hour, cometh the man, or should I say the people? If and when you are truly on your uppers, financial as well as emotional, that is when the folk who really care for you will step to the fore.

Almost a stranger stepped forward, literally and in the most bizarre place to offer a much needed pillar of support.

Whilst queuing for lunch in the palatial dining hall, Phil, a retired officer stepped forward and introduced himself. He explained, with all the mystique of a 'spy in the shadows' movie, and that he may be in a position to help me. Furthermore to meet him in the office after lunch.

Half an hour later he explained that he ran a private training company which specialised in promotion coaching for potential police Sergeants and Inspectors. Also that he had seen me operate in the training environment and was prepared to offer me some work within his company.

A few evenings later as we sat in the empty lecture theatre and went through his proposal, we were also setting the foundations for not only a very fulfilling professional relationship but a lasting friendship too.

The friendship even went on to include an honour he gave me as world class snorer, as we roomed together on a London to Paris charity cycle ride!

I worked for Phil for two or three years on courses both at weekends and in the evenings. It gave me the financial breathing space I needed, and brought business in for his company, a true silver lining indeed.

REUNION

It had been my most positive year since '98. Whilst I still missed Louise I was learning to live without her, and there hadn't been any attacks from either the boys' mum and her legal team or the CSA in relation to maintenance payments. I didn't really expect any but was a little suspicious of the calm that seemed to have enveloped our lives.

With more time to enjoy this 'normality' I began to become restless in wanting to take steps to secure it. I felt that if I didn't, whatever they may be, someone or something would ruin it.

I didn't know what, or how, but like a drug addict desperate for the next hit, I needed to achieve another positive year, and there was only one direction to go.

I'm not a believer in a greater being of any description, but I do however firmly believe that as a parent I have a deep trust in my instinct where the boys are concerned.

Early March, I sat looking out of the office window at the rain, Lewis featuring more than normal in my thoughts that day. It would also be Gavin's fifteenth birthday at the end of the month, to this day I don't know why, but I asked to take an afternoon off as time owed rather than overtime for payment.

This was a perfectly regular thing to do as an option for making best use of my overtime that I'd built up.

I hopped into my car and began the hundred miles or so to Lewis's school. I couldn't contact Lewis but I knew that he was due to leave school that June, and I wasn't prepared to lose contact. I intentionally hadn't told the school I was on my way. I wanted to give him the opportunity to hug me, or hit me, although I didn't think he had anything to hit me for, but I really wasn't too aware of what he felt towards me.

Two hours later I pulled up in the mouth of a small close opposite the main gate. A steady stream, then a flood of kids of all ages poured out. Long hair? Short hair? What kind of fashion? What the hell, I didn't even know what he looked like.

I hadn't been able to get near him for two years, not for wanting to, but I promised him I wouldn't put him in a vice. My heart was racing and I was clammy. I was terrified, but I knew I had to be strong. I'd been strong before and I could do it again.

The flood became a trickle, to droplets. He had either left before, or I missed him and I didn't have a Plan B. I began to drive around the town, the shops, and the estates. Like a policeman stalking a wanted person. He was wanted, so deeply and it was time to show him, beyond doubt, just how much I wanted and loved him.

After thirty minutes or more I decided I stood little chance of finding him like this. So I would leave a note for him at the school reception with my phone number. Let him know I'd

244

tried. It was now Plan C, but at least tomorrow he'd be holding the note I had written. Not the connection I wanted, but better than none, I thought.

Once back at his school I stood in reception, a stranger in a place I should have been familiar with. I explained to the receptionist who cut me off clinically but politely.

"Lewis's head of year is still here, I'll just bleep her for you, please take a seat," pointing to a small alcove of comfortable looking blue seats.

I sat and sweated. What had his head of year been told about me? After what seemed an age, a small group of deep voiced senior year types were huddled around a drinks fountain, just out of view to my left. The accents were all the same, but one had a certain tone, a special tone that was underneath Gavin's voice too. This voice could only belong to one person. As I stood up to walk around the corner, the group appeared and at the front of the group, holding a large artist drawing pad was one stocky, long haired guy. Not the tallest of guys, but then neither am I.

"Lewis?" I said in a cracked and faltering voice.

He stopped and looked straight at me. He swung out his right arm, delivering the pad into the midriff of another group member.

"Hold this," he said in that certain tone.

"You Ok Lewis, who's that?" enquired one of his mates.

"It's my Dad," he said walking the few final steps towards me. Those few steps were finally ending a hellish eight year journey of separation and anguish. His arms clamped shut around me, as did mine around him. Then a moment so treasured, so utterly priceless; as he gently patted me in the centre of the back. Gently patted in the same way I did when he was a baby and toddler, when offering love and support as he grew; now as I patted him again, we showed each other it was all still there.

I sobbed uncontrollably, the receptionist was in tears, and even his buddies bowed their heads for fear of breaking into very un-cool public blubbering!

"Come on, let's go outside." he said.

We walked a little while but the emotion was just too much for me. My legs were shaking and I could hardly talk for sobbing so we sat in the car for a few minutes. During these few first minutes he told me that he doesn't normally stay for that particular after school class, but was doing something for his A level submission. Secondly he wouldn't normally use that route to leave the school, he or one of the group wanted a drink of water. It was as if it was meant to be.

We swapped phone numbers and agreed to meet again soon to chat more and, if necessary, deal with stuff before I told Gavin. We agreed it would be a good time to reunite on Gavin's birthday

He rejoined his mates and as I drove past them towards the school gate there was a smile and a thumbs up. Some two hours later I arrived home. I couldn't help thinking, as I looked and spoke to Gavin that evening that the trip to NYC last birthday

246

was about to be topped, in some style.

The next day, as I arrived for work, a polite enquiry from my boss as to whether all was well,

"Oh yeah" was my simple reply that was disguising a huge feeling of satisfaction and excitement. I was buzzing.

Lewis and I met twice more that month and dealt with quite a lot, but I soon realised that this was only the start of getting to know each other again. A strange concept - father and teenage son getting to know each other, but hell it felt good.

Gavin's birthday arrived, and we were with a few close friends. At a pre-ordained time my phone rang.

"Gavin, it's for you," I said as I handed him my phone.

After the initial look of disbelief, a smile broke across his face and when the tears began to run down his cheek I knew I'd got it right. Exactly a year from wishing, as we jetted off to New York that it would be so lovely if Lewis could join us, he was finally back with us.

Now they just had to meet up again, which I was determined would be soon.

Gavin and I drove to Bracknell for the arranged reunion, in almost silence. The car was filled with nervous anticipation as we were both totally lost in our individual hopes for the future.

At the appointed time Lewis appeared from the train station and into the car park and as he walked towards us I couldn't help drawing the comparison that his steps now, were ending another painful separation, as were his towards me in the school a few weeks ago.

Gavin was in tears and shaking, I was in tears too but rather than shaking I felt strangely calm. Soon they were hugging, then chatting, then laughing; it was great to hear them. The reunion filled me with immense satisfaction but for all concerned was over far too quickly.

As we progressed through the rest of the year, contact between the three of us became more frequent, by phone, e-mail, messenger and visits when convenient. Lewis had a job which involved some weekend work. My first born – working!

Eventually Lewis and his girlfriend Liz were able to come and stay with us for the weekend. For me this was a momentous event, and it was exciting for all of us. It was during the summer and therefore perfect for sitting out on the patio during the balmy evenings. Lewis had in fact been to visit once before for a flying visit but this was special.

I had long dreamed as I battled my adversaries, for evenings such as this. It wasn't unreasonable to wish to spend time with my sons and girlfriends or wives as they grow. It was such reasonable and achievable goals that gave me some hope. It wouldn't have worked to dream of some utopian situation too enormous to achieve in one swoop. Keep it realistic, and then it works, eventually.

One weekend, I collected Lewis and his girlfriend from Bracknell and after a swift drive we were home, Gavin and I trying to contain our excitement whilst Lewis and Liz were trying to relax. I was messing about with patio furniture when I heard Lewis say,

"Dad, got you something."

As he spoke I had a feeling of deep well-being enveloping me. Both sons calling me Dad, in the same place, at the same time, I loved it. As I stepped into the kitchen Lewis was stood there with a bottle of wine for me. White wine in the summer!

Either he had remembered, or taken the time to find out from Gavin, or just a darn lucky guess. Either way I was delighted. It was swiftly chilled and within a couple of hours, used to toast them staying with us.

The wine is long gone but the bottle remains on the welsh dresser in my dining room. I decided to use objects as ornaments that are connected to happy times. I have enough bad stuff stored in the form of legal papers etc. They can gather dust for now in the attic, and in a few years become the subject of a ritual burning.

During this first full weekend visit, I took time out from being busy in the kitchen to just stand and watch the boys messing about in the garden. They were demonstrating very clearly their combined and total inability to use a golf club, for its true purpose. In their collective uselessness they were poking fun, and wielding clubs at each other. There was much laughter, which sounded so sweet.

~

In the August I had to go to court with Louise to get the issue of the house equity resolved. Again, huge legal bills for solicitors doing virtually nothing but trying to turn two people who were once so deeply in love, into enemies. As we walked into court I hated seeing her in these circumstances, almost being painted as enemies. How I would have paid all that money just to hold her hand again. To touch her smooth arms, to see that stunning smile break across her face. How could I possibly fight the woman I still so clearly wanted not to hurt? The hearing was only fifteen minutes and as a result I had re-mortgaged and settled within six weeks. There was no bitterness inside me.

Later that year we raised a glass of wine to a most bizarre ironic twist. Unbeknown to Louise she had engaged the same firm of Solicitors to deal with the property issue, as my ex-wife had used when we first separated! I think I could happily go the rest of my life without another letter bearing that particular logo. Once all was sorted out, I bought her a bottle of her favourite wine. I had no bitterness or ill feeling towards her at all.

However an event before Christmas that was to be bittersweet to the extreme; of course my birthday, forty ninth to be exact. It was Remembrance Sunday, and I had booked a round of golf early, as soon as it was light in fact. I knew the boys had something up their sleeve. How did I know? Gavin is utterly useless at subtlety.

For most of the week running up to my birthday he continually asked me,

"Have you got any plans for your birthday?"

"Yes, golf early" I replied.

"Nothing after?"

"No" I tried desperately not to build myself up, but I just couldn't help it.

I even began to think of how to console myself if they hadn't. Neither had a car, or even a licence, so how could they do anything? I was beginning to beat myself up over this.

It was a beautiful crisp, clear and frosty morning. I tried to concentrate on the orange ball I was using due to the harsh white frost, and as always I put my mobile phone on buzz in my trouser back pocket. Off I went, I knew neither of the boys would be up this early. As I made my way round the course I knew the areas where I could get a signal and those where I wouldn't. Just over half way round my phone went, instead of having the sense to take off my golf glove, I fumbled like an idiot trying to undo the pocket and retrieve my phone.

I pulled out the phone, some loose change, pocket lining, the lot. It was only a slight buzz, just a message, so why the rush anyway? As I looked at the screen I felt beads of sweat gather on my brow despite the below freezing temperature. It was just a number, instead of a name on the screen and I knew the number so well. It was Louise.

Despite all the solicitor generated animosity during the recent property settlement, she still had the niceness to wish me Happy Birthday. At least that's what I hoped the message would say! Indeed it did, I text back a brief thank you message, through a few wistful tears. I wondered if she was missing me as much as I was missing her. My stomach ached as I thought of her.

Then a text from Gavin brought me firmly back into the present, "Be home soon, we are leaving at 12."

"Yes," I looked up to the sky in celebration, hopefully not prematurely.

They have sorted something.

"What" I text back.

His reply was short and to the point; "You'll see, don't be late!" guess that was me told.

By midday I was showered and changed.

Lewis and Liz had moved into their own flat and were having a birthday tea for me with Liz's family coming round too, which was really nice as I hadn't met them yet.

I was walking on air.

Not only were my boys back together, they had organised this for me. I do recall getting home that evening, sitting with a large glass of red and feeling very, very happy.

Sadly, a week or so later the two extremes of my emotions were to collide head on. Gavin was chatting merrily to Lewis on the phone when out of the blue I got a text from Louise asking if she could have a chat. I knew something was wrong. I called and she was crying. I fumbled around trying to get something tidy to put on as she gave me her address, she didn't live far away.

I heard Gavin in the spare room, say "Hang on dads going out."

"What's wrong?" he asked.

"Louise is upset so I'm going to see if I can help her."

"Let me know, give her my love," he shouted as I ran down the stairs and out of the house.

I desperately wanted to have a chat to Lewis but it was more important that he and Gavin continue to communicate.

Ten minutes later I stood trembling on her doorstep. What was I to do? Was she still the same?

As she opened it I stepped in politely, she closed the door. I asked what was wrong and she burst into tears. Instinctively I wrapped her in my arms; she still used the same shampoo! I was in utter turmoil; she was to have surgery over the Christmas and New Year break and had been understandably worried, and a little short of support. As we sat in separate chairs and began talking I could sense that she really needed a hug, but was I the right person anymore?

Try as I did to be strong, I was churning inside and held out my hand and without hesitation she placed her soft hand in mine. I watched as my hand instinctively engulfed hers.

I clearly wasn't the right person to do any more than talk and offer support but I didn't have the heart to tell her it was tearing me apart, she needed me now; I'll deal with me later. I stayed a couple of hours and explained that after our trip to the Highlands I would be home in the first week of January. If she needed anything at all, I would be there for her. Ex-partner maybe but in this instance she was still a friend who needed help, but should that help arrive from other quarters then I would just step back, but until then I would be there for her.

As the year drew on thoughts moved towards Christmas

and what Gavin and I were to do.

Gavin suggested that we forget Christmas, use the money on fuel and go to Scotland, just he, Karle and I. Much as I was delighted at the suggestion, I had just a niggling doubt - was this Gavin's real wish or was he saying what he thought quite rightly, I would want to hear? After a while in thought I recalled all the times he had shown maturity in the past. Why shouldn't he now?

The plan was hatched. Gavin and I would drive to my sisters near Manchester, stay over then continue to Newtonmore on December 21st, Lewis's birthday. Karle would fly to Inverness on Boxing Day then we would all disappear into the wilderness until New Years Eve when we would return to my sister's to toast another fabulous year.

We called Lewis and wished him a Happy Birthday then stopped briefly for a MacDonalds breakfast before the long drive. As we ordered, my phone rang. An unknown number, probably work, but I answered it anyway.

"Hello," I instantly recognised Louise's voice.

"I just wanted to wish you a Happy Christmas and have a lovely time in Scotland." She knew how much I loved the hills and glens. I promised to be in touch as soon as I was back, and if she needed anything, anytime, she was to call.

I remember it wasn't right to wish her a Happy Christmas as she would be worried sick about the upcoming surgery, and she would surely be in pain and discomfort for New Year, so I just wished her well. My heart was beating faster than the car engine for many a mile that day. I was so worried about her, but I couldn't be too close. I had to resign myself that she had asked me for help once already, albeit in the form of a chat and support, so she would ask again if she needed me.

Karle, Gavin and I had a fabulous week in Scotland, especially the last four days when we stayed in a bothy. Bothies are old shepherds shelters maintained for the benefit of walkers, climbers and indeed anyone using the remote areas. The beauty of these is that they are mainly in very remote but stunning locations.

Early on our final day, New Years Eve, I was up just after dawn and nipped outside to take care of the normal morning issue. The sight that greeted me was so beautiful I went straight back and got my camera. It was a sunrise so beautiful, a big red flame coloured sky reaching out towards me contrasted by the harsh, frosted grey and white mountain landscape. These contrasting colours were joined yet somehow softened by a thick band of mist yet to be burned off by the rising sun.

After capturing the view I stood awhile and soaked up the pure majesty of that moment. The boys were still buried in sleeping bags. This was just a moment for me, was it a sign of a good year to come, a good year completed or me just feeling good about life in general? Who knows?

As we walked the nine or so miles back to Dalwhinnie railway station, to the car, and incidentally home of my favourite malt, I felt very positive. I could see the boys ahead of me on their mountain bikes. Even though now it was raining

255

and sleeting with a vengeance, the sunrise was still firmly in my mind. Where did those nine miles go?

Such a lovely feeling back in the car, the heater beginning to make its presence known as we headed south and stopping for coffee at every opportunity. Music, chat and laughter; just the thing to speed up the drive south, and it didn't seem long until we were arriving in Manchester.

I wondered what the New Year would have in store for them and me! New Years Eve for me is about staying in with the boys, or just Gavin of late, watching Jools Holland and looking up to the sky during the transition from one year to another. Not that there are any answers up there! Maybe it's the parallel it draws, the great unknown, as is the year ahead. That mornings stunning sunrise, although only some nineteen hours old seemed a world away.

Happy New Year!

We arrived home in the first week of January 2007. Initially I sent Louise a text letting her know I was home and ready to help in any way I could. I have to admit to a degree of disappointment at not getting an immediate response and requests for help. It was a feeling that I was to endure several times over the coming year. As a caring type person I had become used to people around me, relying on my help and me just being there for them.

Do I text again?

Do I stick my nose in?

Was there now someone close to her who could give all

the help and support she would need during her period of recuperation? It was my instinct to help, usually without request or question but as the days passed by quietly and without reply I assumed that all was well.

I hoped against hope that she wasn't struggling alone, possibly making things more difficult for herself, and feeling awkward about asking for help. All the reasoned argument I employed came back to the same conclusion; there was nothing we didn't know about each other, there was nothing we couldn't talk to each other about and she had already contacted me once. There was no earthly reason why she wouldn't contact me if she needed to. Therefore her silence should be a sign that all was well, a good sign. It didn't however appease me; I was worried sick about her.

I suppose I have to accept that it is just my nature, to care. When the text eventually came towards the end of January it was to help with carrying the shopping. I was pleased, very pleased that she needed me. I turned up to collect her, full of pride and willingness to help. I wasn't however anywhere near prepared for how I felt when she walked, slowly and falteringly from her front door to the car. Her smile was as broad and warm as ever, but I was really rocked by the ungainliness of her movements. I knew it was only temporary but I couldn't help my instinct, to wrap her in my big strong arms. Accepting however that I was no longer the person to do this, was very difficult.

We shopped, we talked, we went to dinner one evening

and met for coffee a time or two over the following month. Maybe this was to see if there was any realistic possibility of rekindling our relationship now that the stress and dark days were for the best part gone. I would be lying if I didn't claim to be nervous, extremely so, at the somewhat bizarre situation we were in. In effect courting the lady I had lived with for six years and whom I had clearly loved so deeply.

Exciting is possibly too strong a word at this early stage but suffice to say it was wonderful, yet nerve wracking, to be back in touch with her. To be seeing her on a regular basis was just so lovely, and I have to say, absolutely normal!

Sadly, after just a few weeks it was clear that we had both moved on and were different people with differing expectations. We had a tearful farewell which was desperately sad. I really didn't know what I had wanted, but I did know that my heart was really aching again at losing her after only a few weeks. I knew I was hurting, but was she? The last thing I wanted was for her to be hurting as I was, but something in me would have felt more satisfied, had she been to some small degree. Was I seeking confirmation that I still meant something to her too?

I wonder if there is anyone out there who will make me feel the way she did, just by walking towards me with a smile breaking across her face. I just wonder…

NATURAL PROGRESSION

Lewis called to tell me that he and Liz were to get married in the coming June I became emotional on several fronts. Firstly I was utterly delighted that he had found that special person in Liz. It was also warming, as the conversation went on, to learn than Liz and he had been friends, then true friends for several years before dating. During these years Liz had been one of the people close to him and had given him immense support during some very troubled times. Now that friendship and support had turned and progressed to love, I knew his heart and soul were in safe hands.

Secondly, I looked forward with relish to help guide him through the next phase of his life. I had missed so much of his teenage years and although I couldn't make up for that, I ached inside for the opportunity to help him and indeed them.

Finally, when he explained they didn't want a showcase wedding costing thousands because they already had a flat and wanted to save for their own house, I knew they were approaching the future sensibly. I took immense confidence from that.

We chatted and it was soon very clear that they had thought this one through with maturity. It was in no way a display of impatience. My feelings of uncertainty soon gave way to pride, followed by a horrific feeling of, "What if I hadn't got in touch?" I would have missed all this. The thought of him getting married and me not knowing was too unpleasant to even consider. Anyway, "Stop it" I had to tell myself. He would have told me no matter what, "Stop it."

When I eventually settled to the idea I was so full of pride and love, and my thoughts turned to being a grandad, who knows. I felt it was too early and possibly untactful to ask their plans but a huge sense of pride filled me when I realised exactly what being a grandad would mean to me personally. To the children of Lewis and Liz, and in time Gavin, I would be referred to as Grandad Reed. I am struggling for words to adequately express the feelings of pride and emotion triggered in me by those two words.

To be 'Grandad Reed,' would place me almost at the top of my world. My esteem would be at its highest possible level. I would be joining this elite group of individuals, and in doing so have achieved something I longed for.

The most immediate member of that club is sadly gone, my Dad, Jack. A man who was humble yet proud, who made mistakes but had the decency to admit them rather than seeking to blame any passing circumstance or person. A man who for many reasons I admired greatly and I, like a lot of teenage boys, argued with so much in my adolescent years, but as I grew through those turbulent times and into my twenties I eventually realised that he really had been there for me and really did know what he was talking about!

To stand alongside him, and share his title would be an honour. I still feel, deep in the pit of my stomach, a sense of loss so profound that tears instantly well in my eyes. I may well be in my fifties, big and strong enough to deal with most things, but I still miss him so much.

My Grandad enriched my childhood in so many simple but priceless ways. Visiting or even staying with him was pure boys own adventure. Whether it was searching in his bureau for the hidden Mars bars or tubes of Smarties, or rolling around the open woodlands in the Wythenshawe area of Manchester as between us, we repelled the surging flow of red Indians. He was the best deputy this sheriff ever had!

I have a photo at home of my passing out parade at Aldershot in 1976 on completion of my two year Army apprenticeship. In this particular picture he is there, quietly but proudly watching. My family were fortunate enough to have seats at the front of the stands so my Dad and Grandad were there to see me pass out. Both being ex-military men, their pride was tangible. It was a memorable day, but sadly they are both gone now. I look forward to being a very proud bearer of the title they both shared.

~

One normal car washing day, Gavin appeared at the side of the garage, not only to enjoy watching my labours but to make a rather important announcement.

"I've been looking at the website and thinking about it for

261

a while; I want to join the Navy."

I was stunned, delighted and with pride surging through me, also a soapy sponge dripping all over my foot.

"I know you were in the Army but I just fancy the Navy more."

Bless him, the second sentence was spoken with some nervousness, as if he was expecting my reaction to be negative. I was so delighted, more so as he had arrived at this decision alone. He knew I had fond memories of my time in the Army. There are some pictures around the house, not many, but sufficient to express my enjoyment, and a degree of pride.

"Ok, what are you going to do about it," was my response, quickly followed by me confirming my total delight at his decision.

Even quicker was my explanation that my delight was for his future, not my peace and quiet! He had decided to go to the recruiting office the following Tuesday. He had a plan already!

Announcement over, he went about his normal weekend routine, sleeping, eating and going out 'Pillocking.'

This now needs some explanation; 'Pillocking' was a name I chose to describe a predominantly teenage male pastime. It simply involves sitting in a small car, usually more guys than there are seats for. The car won't be driving anywhere because collectively they haven't any money for fuel. The car usually has one or two outriders. These extreme form of Pillockers sit on their scooters which are raised onto centre stands. They wear their crash helmets high on the back of their heads in a failed attempt to look cool. The car has to be fitted with an obscenely large sound system. The system, when duly switched on makes conversation an ancient art form, except to grunt in a Stone Age manner as each person takes their turn to fart. Obviously the effects are that much more intense due to the sardine tin conditions in the car. This all takes place on the forecourt of a local garage or public car park, and when observed from a safe distance all you hear is a deep bass beat, a total absence of accompanying melody and a car full of teenage Neanderthals nodding their heads and exchanging self-approving glances. Looking like a right bunch of pillocks!

Don't get me wrong, as a father and a police officer, pillocking is infinitely better than doing drugs or committing crime. Pillocking should be embraced, not shunned, as it is ultimately there for the entertainment of the more stable members of society.

A few days after Gavin's announcement about the Navy I endured a very nervous day at work knowing he was at the recruiting office. I wondered whether he would be treated seriously as he wasn't quite sixteen. My worries, although perfectly natural, were unfounded. He arrived home with a bag full of goodies, a DVD containing an insight into the many ways of transferring his particular brand of carnage onto a world stage and, importantly, he had a date for his entrance exam.

He sailed, (ooh pardon the pun) through the test and was given a date for a medical and finally an interview. All went well and the day of the interview arrived. I sat in the car in a parking space in Queens Square, Bristol, waiting patiently and nervously for him.

I had worked in this area for eleven years based at the Central Police Station nearby and as I watched a ballet of busy lives being performed all around, I drifted off down memory lane, lots of good memories. Suddenly I was aware of a young man walking towards me, one of many people in this crowded part of town. Black polished shoes, smart jeans, pink checked shirt and black suit jacket. As he neared the car, a smile broke across his face, he looked down as if in some embarrassment and very subtly made a thumbs up gesture with both hands at forty five degrees to his thighs. This was no longer the young boy I had guided and brought up, not the sad and frustrated schoolboy battling with past emotions. This was a tall, presentable, developing young man beginning to take charge of his own destiny.

"I'm in," he croaked as he got into the car.

We hugged in silence. This was just so special, to me, special to him, special because he had succeeded this far on his own. He had a four day boot camp assessment to attend in Scotland later in the year, but to all intents and purposes, he was in. The Navy wanted him and I felt so proud.

NEW DIRECTIONS

April 2007 saw a reality check for me. I was on a pre-retirement course which emphasised I was really getting close to the end of my service.

Although I had no desire to remain in or with the police service, I am happy to leave with generally good memories and my pension intact!

In June as I drove to my hotel near Farnborough on the eve of Lewis and Liz's wedding, I was washed over time and time again by waves of differing emotions. Gavin had travelled up to stay with Lewis a few days earlier so I had only my own thoughts for company. By the following evening I would have a daughter in law, Liz. I'd known Liz and her family for just over a year. As I don't live close I didn't see them on a day to day basis so getting to know Liz and her family was a slow but pleasant process. What I did know however was that even though we had spent several years apart, I still knew Lewis very well. He was happy, and that, as any parent feels, will do for me.

Not being a particularly formal person, and it being late June. I decided on a biscuit coloured linen suit, brown shoes and a basically white shirt with a faint blue and pink stripe, but no tie. I felt I may get stick from the other quarters for being a little informal but it was Ok by Lewis and Liz, so that's all that mattered.

My job for the day was to collect, Lewis, Bruce (his best man and best mate) and Gavin as usher and little bruv from their flat and drive them to the church. They looked resplendent in their black suits, white wing collared shirts and champagne coloured waistcoats and cravats.

Guess what?

I blubbed as soon as I saw them, I had a surprise for Lewis. Unbeknown to him I had contacted his other Gran and had a card from her. I asked him to read it, with Liz – later that day. The church service went well, during which I sat quietly at the rear not wishing to cause friction between me and his mum.

The rights and wrongs of my decision to take a lower key role than many fathers at a sons wedding can be debated for many an hour. However, had friction occurred and tarnished Lewis and Liz's memory of this day, regardless of whoever caused it, would have been unforgivable. There were one or two comments about my low key role but not only did they not know I had discussed this with Lewis, but more importantly they didn't see a deeply moving gesture as Lewis and Liz made their way slowly to sign the register. As he passed me, he subtly put his hand on my shoulder, gave it a firm squeeze and then a couple of quick pats. It was his way of privately stating his acceptance of my role. I was very pleased and immensely proud. I reached into my pocket for my handkerchief.

The reception encapsulated the feelings of the whole day, as well as the personalities of bride and groom. The overriding emotion was joy. The overriding gesture was a smile, and as Lewis later wrote in a letter to his grandma in Taunton, it all went really well, even Mum and Dad were in the same room for five hours without war breaking out! Thus justifying, my decision to be low key. I was as I have always been, silently in the background, but always there.

There were many tears, but all of happy emotion from me, there's a surprise then, and from Gavin, who was so happy to see Lewis content. That evening and with all the partying in full swing, and destined to remain so well into the night I drove my sister, Gavin and two nephews back to the hotel. We sat out in the garden and had a few drinks to round the day off.

It began to rain but the huge patio umbrella kept us dry and my feelings simply couldn't be dampened. My gift to them was a honeymoon. It was an expense they would have made do without, but is so needed after the stressful build up to the big day. I drove them to Gatwick the following day, hoping their week in Tunisia would be just what they needed to relax.

Early July and with the wedding a fond memory, I sat in the office looking forward to the summer. Gavin had finished college with the units he needed to complete the course. As my mind wandered, the office phone rang as if to interrupt my warm moment; I answered in normal work style to hear a long term colleague,

"Hi Geoff, Paul here." A guy I worked with before going

into the training world and who like me became a trainer after many years an operational officer.

"Geoff, I've been asked to call and tell you that sadly Paul Mallet has died."

Shock, "How?" I shouted

He relayed some words meaning brain tumour and infection to me.

"Ok, I'll call you back" I put the phone down.

Why? How? Why him? Why my friend Paul?

So many scum bags still breathing and Paul had gone.

No!

I'm not really sure what I was saying or how loud I was saying it but the ladies from the next office came in to see what was wrong. They looked sad, but confused, they didn't know of Paul or his meaning to me. How he had propped me up when I needed, gave me direction and got me drunk when I needed too.

I had only been speaking to him a few weeks earlier and he sounded so utterly comfortable, relaxing with his partner Justin after a wild night out in Cardiff.

I rang my boss to tell her I needed to go home, this was a devastating blow. I needed to tell Gavin, and begin to come to terms with such a loss myself. Paul wasn't just a friend, albeit a dear friend, he was family to me.

"I know Geoff, it's about Paul. You go home and take whatever time you need."

The guy who called to tell me of Paul's death had pre warned my boss and I was so grateful for that foresight.

Paul had been so pleased at Gavin's Navy acceptance, so pleased for us both and always so generous in his praise of me. Praise I found difficult to accept, but knew it was given totally sincerely. Immediately I called Louise. She was the only person I wanted to call, my instinct. She offered to come and sit with me. I said I would be Ok but really wish I had said yes. She was very fond of Paul too. Maybe we could have helped each other come to terms with it.

He can't possibly be dead, he's not even forty.

I drove home after texting Gavin to be at home.

He stood silent as I told him, ashen-faced in disbelief. Fortunately he let tears flow, which was positive in that he felt comfortable letting his feelings show. We hugged each other in support at the loss of someone so dear to us both. Our loss of course was minimal compared to that of Justin, his partner, or Paul's daughter and of his family. Not only had the police service lost a fine officer it had lost a truly inspirational trainer.

Diversity is a massive and positive subject to be celebrated. I don't just mean skin colour, religion or cultural issues. The real worth of diversity is too often lost when abused by so say experts, with personal agendas, trying to beat society into trying to see life from their own angle. It simply isn't that, it's about opening your eyes and your mind. It's about being receptive towards a huge raft of issues, for example age, mobility, social issues such as perceived class, I could go on. I consider myself utterly privileged to have seen and indeed shared some of Paul's finest hours.

If he had a weakness at all, it was his selfless devotion to others, sometimes to the detriment of himself. How many nights did he sit well into the early hours with me, instead of getting to sleep himself? At work he was as immaculate in appearance, as he was sharp of mind.

The rest of that warm July day I sat on a bench overlooking a long fairway and lake at the golf club. There were professionals there, practicing for an event. It should have been good to watch the pro's, but I barely saw them. I asked Gavin if he wanted to come with me, he didn't, but started his grieving process his way, with his own friends. We exchanged brief but supportive texts during the afternoon.

Gavin and I had individual memories of Paul as well as collective ones. We could deal with the collective ones at home, in the evening or on our travels. The individual ones however required time dedicated to Paul's memory. To shed some tears, to spend time with his spirit, as he had spent time with us. I spent the whole of the next day on the same bench. I loved Paul in a way so deep, and am so full of gratitude. Slowly it sank in that I'd never see him again, the pain was so intense.

When my Dad died in 2001, I hurt differently and I still miss him today. He was so fed up with taking tablets. The indignity of the medical treatment just to keep him living, but not alive, was appalling. I last saw him alive in a bed on a ward of strangers at Thameside Hospital, he had no dignity, nor quality of life. When I left he shed a tear, as did I. So when dad went my deep sadness was eased slightly in the knowledge that

270

as a proud man he was now released from pain and indignity.

Paul's death however was such a massive shock. Yes, I knew he had been ill with a brain related illness a year or more before, but I had seen him since, back at work, enjoying life.

Funerals are sad events, fact! You don't go to one looking for a good time, although I have sometimes left them feeling somewhat drunk. However Paul's in his home town of Caerphilly was an event of deep, profound sadness, yet pride too. It gave a very clear message to the whole town that this funeral was of a person who had truly contributed in so many positive ways to people and to helping them, not only nationwide but internationally too.

All the traffic lights in the town centre were switched to red. Everything stopped as Paul made his final trip, escorted by motorcyclists from Gwent Police and South Wales Police. The streets leading to the church were lined by police officers from many forces across Wales and England. Officers whose careers Paul had already had an impact on. I walked towards the church but, despite my usual promptness, was too late to get inside before Paul arrived. I stood in silence watching what was possibly, his personal farewell. The hearse pulled up at the gate, I stood about ten metres away watching the coffin bearers place him on their shoulders. Finally, one of the funeral directors, carefully, placed Paul's cap on the Gwent Police flag which adorned his coffin. Placed carefully and immaculately, reflecting the sunshine from the polished peak. He was still shining.

Gavin, realising what his hat symbolised looked straight at me. I think he was trying to ask if I was Ok. Too late; my eyes flooded, my stomach wretched and my legs trembled. I raised my hand to my mouth, but I don't know why. We followed the coffin party into the church, walking the final few yards with him, a huge honour.

As the eulogy was being read by a senior officer, one part has remained with me. Paul had done a lot of child protection work and it was mentioned that there were many children who had been helped in so many ways by Paul, at this point Gavin started to turn towards me and said in a cracked low whisper,

"And I'm one of them," then buried his head in my shoulder.

We cried openly, as did many others in the church on that very sad day.

GAVIN'S OWN VOICE

Summer of 2007 wasn't spectacular by any means, but it did allow some time to sit outside, enjoy a barbeque and a few glasses here and there and allow my mind to drift.

Paul's death had clearly devastated us, but we began to talk about him gradually which I took to be a positive sign. I started to take stock of where I was, what was going on in my life, where the boys were heading and where I was going, with less than a year to retirement.

I reflected back to 'The Great Outdoors Challenge' that I sadly had to resign from with that foot infection. The Highlands have long been a place of relaxation, source of strength and inspiration as well as huge mental and physical challenges for me over the years.

It was the prophetic words of the doctor at Kingussie when digging the infection out of my foot, "The challenge is over for you," that really became a focal point. Words I have repeated to myself countless times over the ensuing years as many challenges laid before me have been faced and overcome. It is ironic that all the deep aching pain that I as a parent; and indeed all parents potentially or actually go through tear us to shreds we would without hesitation endure again and again. Emotional

273

wounds so deep that our lives simply cannot be the same because they change us as people; leave scars so hideous it's as if the whole world is looking at us with grotesque fascination.

Perhaps paranoia and the truth is far different, but these wounds and scars are buried deep within ourselves and we alone choose what others see.

The more I have opened up to myself, the deeper the wounds and scars may be but I am the only one who is fully aware of them. Sadly, there's no surface gloss or decoration we can use to screen ourselves from their effects as we wear a brave face that fools everyone around us, except the closest to us who suffer hugely too.

When I sit and reflect on the progress the boys have made, all my hurt and trauma just seems to fade to a minor discomfort. By progress I mean not just school, college, work, housing etc. but the way they in turn deal with the little, or not so little nasties life begins to throw at them. In particular in March 2007, when Reading County Court allowed his mother to make an application forcing Gavin to visit her.

As ugly and repulsive a standpoint as this was, again it was the system that allowed it. Gavin was sixteen years old nearing six foot tall and with a voice as deep as a ships horn. Couple these factors with extreme intelligence and eloquence, then you have Gavin explaining his terms as to when and if he visits his mother. That is the beauty, if it can be called that, of the Children's Act proceedings, that the children either directly or indirectly have a voice albeit the extent and method used to convey their feelings depends on age. Listening to Gavin as he spoke politely but firmly to the judge I felt immense pride in that he was behaving rationally, in a very emotionally charged situation. I could feel many years of anger and frustration on his behalf being at last released, and in the perfect situation. I quietly thought to myself, 'Go for it boy, but stay in control of your mouth.' He did so, and as we left that room I couldn't help feeling that I had led a child in, but was now leaving with a young man.

So beware trying to indoctrinate the children, however subtle you think you are. The truth of the children's feelings will come out and the persons who may try the emotional route will ultimately have some very awkward questions to answer regarding their motives later.

In the first hearing Gavin spoke directly to the judge, un-phased and wholly in control of himself, boiling with anger and indignation on the inside but calm, accurate and deliberate on the outside. Application refused. Whilst Gavin still had some issues to deal with, as do all teenagers emerging into young men, this was a clear demonstration to all that he was becoming his own person.

A concept I was to struggle with later that year too. We argued several times over a particularly stormy autumn and winter, when he began hanging around with some folk I didn't care too much for. I had to really concentrate on reigning myself in on occasions. Gavin was now making his own way, or starting to, I had to step back a little and allow him to progress as well as make mistakes. Similar to when they are learning to walk, watching them stumble and fall every few steps. Successfully putting three or four paces together before reaching for the sofa edge which sadly is just out of reach, and another moment of almost triumph ends in a face to face with the carpet.

I found stepping back so very difficult, my protective instinct being so powerful had served us both so well over the years and I couldn't come to terms with ignoring it. Not being able to sleep until he was in at night; even though he would then watch TV into the small hours but, at least he was home. He would react in frustration then I would react to his apparent disregard to everything I say. Turbulent would be an understatement, then I'd go back to self-examination. They, the boys, are still and always will be at my very core and I'm sure that as time moves on I'll find it easier to step back, but I would rather be the father I am than not have the protective and guiding instincts that I do.

One thing guaranteed to enrage me is when I hear a parent accepting a situation that clearly isn't in the best interests of the children but they allow it to go unchallenged, and usually thinking,

"But what can I do? He, or she, has got a solicitor." Sadly very common, and more likely a lack of knowledge that a solicitor is source of information to stand for your rights, remember you employ them and they take instructions. The solicitor is employed to state which options are available to you within the law. Then make sure that whatever process is being followed; is followed correctly, again within the law. It is such a shame though, for society as a whole, that rarely does family law's horrendous bias towards the mother get challenged.

There are just as many good Dads as good Mums.

TO MY INDEPENDENCE!

November 2007, my birthday month and not just any birthday, it was my fiftieth. This was to be a milestone I had awaited eagerly for many years, I don't know why but I just did. November 12th was the day and exactly six months from my retirement. My retirement was however to be anything but the popular image of retirement, but it was to be a pivotal point in my life.

The boys were well on their way in life and although I relished the dad role and, hopefully grandad in the future, I was now moving into a new role of being free to do pretty much as I wanted.

I naturally became less of a hands on dad as the boys matured into adults and was now fully confident in leaving Gavin at home if I had a weekend away. This was a massive step, considering all the child protection issues in the past, but it has to be done if only to show that the increased maturity being shown is getting rewarded with trust.

So, with the weekends expanding into longer periods of independence, I began to make plans for my retirement. I felt almost guilty to begin with, making plans with neither of them in.

How selfish was I becoming?

This was a question I mused over for quite some time but eventually arriving at a peaceful place, where I had accepted that I wasn't being selfish at all. I was in fact acting purely naturally, it just took me a while to realise it. Having arrived at this utopian state of mind and whilst walking around work with a permanent smile I wandered into my friend Kevin's office, deep within the technical dungeons of Police HQ.

"Yer, Geoff, you like going to out of the way cheap places, like me, don't you?" Kev said in his Bristolian accent!

"Yeah, where?" I replied.

"Poland and Ukraine."

"You're pissed"

"No serious, there's a budget airline Bristol to Eastern Poland and blag a cheap taxi to Lviv, in the Ukraine, Lviv is the Ukraine's second city."

"When?" I asked.

'Monday 12th to 16th November."

"That's my birthday the 12th, I must be pissed too, but count me in."

Within an hour, the phone calls and bookings were made for a trip to celebrate my fiftieth birthday plus the reawakening of my own independence. This was to be, however a trip that was also to see me and Kev flirt with danger to a degree far surpassing anything in my previous fifty years and indeed danger from an unimaginable source.

In the early evening Monday 12th November, we found

ourselves in the bar at Bristol Airport. I was getting acquainted with a large glass of red whilst Kev being a connoisseur of chemically manufactured, and in my personal opinion, tasteless beers, was doing his best to enjoy a pint of bitter.

Gavin was ok, in fact more than happy at having the house to himself for four days. What sixteen year old guy wouldn't? Soon we were aboard our flight to Rzeszow, in Eastern Poland. If you can read this and follow us on an online map or the like, it may give a clearer picture of our adventure and indeed the emotion.

I was still a little self-conscious about the four inch diameter bright yellow and pink 'I'm 50 today' badge adorning my shirt but I'd promised to wear it and a promise is a promise!

A little over two hours later, and that's more than enough on a budget flight, we landed at Rzeszow. It was very dark and really, really cold! A kind of cold we don't get in the UK. After an efficient small airport experience we were in a taxi towards the town centre. Then comes the first foul- up; Hotel room for Kev, none for Geoff! It's my birthday still, so I pleaded with the staff to find me a room despite the,

"We are full." protests of the staff!

However the birthday spirit was alive and well and,

"We don't have a twin room, only two singles," was the eventual offer from the receptionist.

"It is paid for your friend, but you," icily pointing a scarily manicured nail at me, "must pay now also for a room."

"Ok" I replied. I was tired hungry and in need of a beer so

agreed without much of a fight. We trudged up the stairs to the rooms which were virtually opposite each other and, like a scene from a Brian Rix farce, we both reappeared in the corridor within seconds,

"There's two F****** beds in here" we both said before inspecting each other's room, to find the single rooms did in fact have two beds in each. Exasperated laughter echoed along the corridor as we locked up and wandered downstairs and out in search of food and a couple of drinks. Not forgetting to fix the receptionist a death stare as I passed her.

Out into the seriously cold night we ventured but imagine our delight to see an outdoor café within a hundred metres, with stand-to tables and patio heater style lamps inside a snow umbrella.

Having ordered what I thought was a baguette style pizza and fries I was delighted to be handed almost that. A bit of green pickled veg here and there but on the whole pretty close so I tucked in, soon to be joined by Kev with similar offerings and, unfortunately, one of the local drunks on a scavenging foray from the nearby railway station. I wasn't really sure if he was asking me for a few of my chips, stupid idea, or some money, even more stupid, to get his own food or more drink. Either way the answer was the same,

"No!"

He became a little persistent and claimed he didn't understand English. If he didn't understand English then how on earth did he know I was speaking it?

However when I delivered my answer with sufficient venom I was mightily impressed at his sudden grasp of colloquial English! We ate our fill, much to the drunk's disgust, and then wandered through the town eventually having a couple of welcome beers at a really pleasant bar. Rzeszow was a town I warmed to despite the six inches of snow and constant subzero temperatures. This was rural Poland and I had instantly taken it to heart. My new found independence was beginning to feel good too.

Next morning after a café breakfast of eggs, bacon and bread with coffee, we boarded a train for Przemsyl. A journey of approximately seventy miles due east which took a little under two hours. This was to take us to a rendezvous with a bus for a short drive to the border crossing point at Medyka, where we would finally enter Ukraine.

The train was old rolling stock, but perfectly suited to the grey harshness of the poorly maintained buildings. The countryside was covered with a thick layer of snow and topped by a weighty grey sky, providing a truly atmospheric journey further east. Barely a hill to be seen, flat as far as the eye could see, divided neatly by telegraph poles, cables and power pylons and dotted by farms and infrequent signs of habitation.

Kev and I were the only ones in our compartment which was strangely private as we travelled ever east, eventually arriving at Przemsyl. Kev had read the guide books, researched the journey and all in all done his homework well, so how we managed to get off a stop too early is still a mystery!

The town has an outer, as well as a central station, so we chose the outer, of course! We stood like a pair of tools on a bleak, snow covered station surrounded by un-inspiring concrete panel blocks of flats, obvious communist era leftovers, but strangely solid and warm looking amid such harsh surroundings. We caught another train within a few minutes to the central station, and back on our route.

We walked a few hundred metres, still blindly following Kev's directions, to a truly memorable car park at the rear of the station and boarded a minibus for Medyka. The first real sign of just how far east we were was the street and bus sign written in the Cyrillic alphabet.

Along with another forty or so souls we crushed onto the twenty seater mini-bus for the short but scary white knuckle ride to the border with Ukraine. Health and safety isn't an issue here, and when eventually arriving at the border our well-travelled eyes were to behold a scene which left us both speechless. What a place this was. Like a gold rush, or wild west trading post town without the quiet, good order and respect for diversity!

Kev had decided we would cross into the Ukraine on foot, as the locals do. Experience the reality of this place as oppose to a slick, glitzy tourist crossing point or airport. Stepping off the bus was to enter a truly alien world. There were a variety of colourfully painted huts with v-shaped roofs like seaside changing huts, but this was no pretty seaside resort, it was dirty, it was grey and it was desperate. The ground was littered with

283

empty cigarette cartons which had been discarded almost in open defiance of the laws governing import into Ukraine.

We were still on the Polish side, still being the word. Stood rooted and staring open mouthed at the chaos around us. Kev and I must have shone out like beacons as wealthy western tourists ogling at their life. Wearing our normal UK High Street clothes and with one hundred US dollars in my wallet, I felt very wealthy, and very threatened.

Three ladies stood on the pavement ten yards ahead of us who began to shout at us. They didn't seem angry but I suppose I felt it as anger because I was looking at their world like some drug fuelled dream. We began to walk towards them, only because I recognised a hand-written sign on a hut behind them; bank/exchange in poorly formed letters. The foyer of this bank was oh so different, room for two at best, about the size of your average toilet cubicle. As we approached the ladies I said to Kev,

"Do you think they are toms (prostitutes) out here, in this cold,"

He snapped, "Don't talk bollocks."

I suppose he had a point so I shut up.

I nervously pushed a twenty dollar note under the cashier screen, no forms to fill in and as I tried to smile confidently I felt decidedly nervous. I couldn't help feeling that if this went wrong, to this stone faced and hair lacquered vision before me, the fact that I was a British police officer wasn't going to cut much ice!

Before I got my Ukraine currency I was unceremoniously bundled aside by a granny from hell. I have no idea what she was saying but it sure didn't sound like, "Excuse me sir" as she launched some money at the cashier who quick as a flash produced about ten packets of cigarettes and slid them under the screen in single file and into a waiting plastic bag.

I had the distinct feeling that these two had done this before. So entranced by these goings on I was still staring at the fast departing granny when the cashier rattled the Perspex screen, she forced a huge bundle of bank notes through to me. I tried to calculate quickly; twenty dollars equals about ten pounds so these notes must be worth oooh about ten pence each. My final display of complete ineptitude was when I gestured to the cashier, with a flick of my right hand, do I have to sign anything. I got the head tilted to the side and a, don't be a dick head smile.

Kev was still outside in the snow.

"What took you so long," he said.

"If you could have done any better!" I gave him half the Ukrainian money, good job he brought a rucksack!

The border crossing was a tunnel system of high metal fences, all painted a dull green. We walked about five hundred metres until we reached another dull grey building. The path stopped at the aluminium framed door. Whilst walking this path we saw countless people stuffing packet after packet of cigarettes into their clothing. Being easier to conceal in small packets than in cartons of two hundred, the cartons all over the road near the huts made sense now.

We moved through in groups of about six or eight people at a time. The Polish were polite, even friendly. Once out of Poland there was a short walk to a similar hut, which had a pale blue and yellow flag above it, and inside there began Ukraine.

As she looked at me coldly the Ukraine police officer had deep mistrust in her eyes. I don't think it was personal, maybe just that neither I, nor Kev, handed her a couple of packets of cigarettes on the way through, or maybe she just wasn't happy with her job that day.

The whole process was alarmingly quick, taking half an hour maximum until we appeared, out of the maze of footpaths on the Ukraine side. Now this was desperate!

We accepted a taxi of sorts to take us the sixty miles or so to Lviv, again due east along a poorly maintained road through very grey countryside. The image of poverty was made more intense as we passed through small villages and eventually the outskirts of Lviv, as people shuffled through grey snow or crammed onto ageing buses spewing clouds of dark grey smoke. We arrived at the hotel two hours later, and very gratefully too. The nice Volkswagen taxi had so many faults and rattles it didn't need a radio. The journey was topped off by the oil pressure alarm sounding and the driver just pulled the fuse out whilst driving instead of maybe stopping and putting oil in, and carried on at the same reckless speed!

Lviv was a beautiful city. Very powerful and thought provoking architecture. The locals were friendly towards us but, whenever there were official procedures to comply with, the bureaucracy was stifling and always carried out with an air of mistrust. Whether this was a left over from the communist era I don't know but having travelled through East Germany as it was in the early eighties, it certainly felt like it. Here's hoping that with the generations the mistrust will decrease and increased openness will develop. We stayed two nights and had a really good time, despite real language issues and freezing temperatures, even in the midday sun.

Our second night we decided to go for a quiet couple of beers, however on our return we didn't realise that the hotel locked its doors about midnight. So arriving back a little after that, we made our way through the small courtyard at the front, to the main door. We tried to call the number on the door but our phones wouldn't connect to the local network. It was minus five degrees Celsius, and not wanting to spend the night outside we knocked on the glass door to wake the staff. This didn't work and after several attempts we were getting concerned. We didn't have suitable clothes for a night in this weather. A couple more attempts to wake the staff, the step-through door in the courtyard wall opened and a police officer walked in. In broken English he asked what we were doing.

After explaining our predicament I pointed at the phone number on the door and asked him to call for us. He looked at us for a second or two, then, to my astonishment said,

"No" and walked briskly out of the courtyard.

We were stunned.

Thoughts of a walk around the city were rejected after looking at the neon temperature display in the main square. It was getting even colder. We sat in the two chairs in the courtyard and discussed making some form of shelter out of the chairs and some builder's rubble, laying across the courtyard.

The step through door opened again and the policeman re-appeared, this time with three or four others one of whom had red epaulettes on the shoulders of his very warm looking coat. Three chrome stripes on his epaulettes, like a sergeant and it was clear that the he was in charge. He spat out some orders, and we were instantly made to stand and face separate walls. My hands were spread wide and placed on the wall in front of me, my legs spread and I assumed the same was happening to Kev, although I couldn't see him.

Next, to our horror, the officer standing very close to my right produced his handgun. He held it close to the side of my right shoulder, not against my head but close enough for me to see it. It was shiny and oily, well maintained and I had no doubt it would work. I still couldn't see Kev but I now know he was getting the same treatment to my left.

Then another officer took everything out of my pockets. Wallet, change, passport, phone, the lot. The sergeant appeared to my left and sat in one of the chairs Kev and I had been using earlier. He was about a yard from me. I saw as he sat he had all my things, and Kev's, in his hands.

"You criminals?" he asked in a deep and abrupt manner.

"No, English Police, on holiday" I replied.

He proceeded to check passports and rummage through our wallets. He would glance up at me every few seconds and could see I was really scared now.

Eventually he stood up, and after a short while put all our belongings on the chair.

The guns were put away and we turned to face them. I still wanted to ask for help and as I started to talk, the sergeant came face to face with me. He was literally nose to nose and his breath was foul. He pointed at me,

"You shhh or," then made a hand shape of a pistol and a quiet verbal mimicking of a gun being fired.

We both agreed this a really good time to shhhhhhhhhh!

Then they were gone, so were the U.S Dollars that had been in our wallets. The filthy bastards had robbed us. The Police had robbed two of their own. I was fuming yet powerless. Who do we report it to? We just needed to get out of this country, soon.

We paced the courtyard until about six o'clock when MacDonalds opened, yes they have them too, we gulped hot coffee. They had stolen our dollars but not their crappy worthless currency.

About eight o'clock we got back into the hotel and explained what had happened but to our amazement the receptionist simply raised her eyebrows and said in very clear English,

"Not again."

After a quick visit to a money exchange, luckily we had

some US dollars in our room, we were in the taxi speeding towards the border, although the driver smoked like a chimney, the car was sound. We were both tired but I just couldn't sleep, maybe adrenalin, maybe the seething anger within me at being robbed by my own profession.

Once at the border we bribed the guards with twenty dollars, and with the help of a fixer who turned out to be the multi-talented taxi driver who had picked us up on the way in, we were back in Poland within an hour, very quick compared to the poor souls who queue for three or more hours each day just to go to work.

That trip to Ukraine, and in particular the fifteen minutes or so at the hands of the Ukrainian Police made me realise again that the freedoms we take for granted in the west are hard won, and indeed precious. Although the legal system needs to take a long look at itself in my opinion, it is still able to be challenged unlike, I would imagine, the Ukrainian system.

My dearest wish is that the boys know all of what has happened, so that they have the confidence if one day they feel they are being subjected to an injustice, to challenge it, but always in a correct and safe manner.

LETTING GO

My wish began to show itself over the Christmas and New Year holiday period.

Gavin and I travelled to stay with Lewis and Liz in the run up to the holidays. It was very clear that they were well on the way with preparations for the festivities, clearly a Christmas of their own organising. They would see who they wanted, when they wanted and even had planned a party for their friends. I sat proudly, watching as they went about their preparations, shopping, wrapping and above all discussing. It was good to hear their mum mentioned. The last thing I ever wanted was them to feel that they couldn't mention her in my presence. It was always my desire that they should have freedom of speech as well as thought.

After a few lovely days with them it was time to leave and travel home. Going home was always going to be sad but like millions of other parents it is tinged with satisfaction at seeing them make their own ways in a positive manner based on their own values. It's also, if I am allowed a little self-back patting, hugely satisfying to see traces of the values I tried to display in there too.

The holiday period at home however, was one of a starker

realisation and yet equal pride. I had as always planned to do nothing but be with Gavin. He on the other hand had oh so many things planned!

I had singularly and if I am to be honest spectacularly failed to notice that he was a fit, healthy, near six foot tall sixteen and three quarter year old with a whole different agenda for the festive period. There was of course festive pillocking to be enjoyed. Maybe a party or two, festive out and about stuff and not forgetting of course plenty of festive better not let dad know where I have been tonight stuff.

My initial feelings of frustration that I seemed to spending this holiday season alone on the sofa were again pacified when I asked myself why. Pacified by the realisation that he was out there doing what most guys his age do. It also kept the food consumption rate low. It was really difficult at first to accept his increasing independence; however I had plenty of time most evenings to contemplate why I was finding it so difficult.

Eventually I arrived at a conclusion of sorts. It was me really struggling to allow him to begin making his own, different, mistakes. I wondered whether other parents felt the same, especially at releasing the youngest child. Were these feelings, my feelings, those of redundancy creeping in and in so doing was it fuelling my disillusionment?

I had to get over this final hurdle and quickly, I mustn't let it damage or hinder either of our development. To do this I decided to fit my own life into a fairly predictable regime. Not ignoring him but maybe just shifting the balance of attention back to me a little and hopefully showing him I was giving him space.

I changed my daily routine and found some areas more difficult than others, for instance if he didn't get home or chose to go elsewhere after work his tea would be plated and left for him. This turned out to be immensely difficult for me, as a chef before being a police officer and for several years being insistent that he ate a proper tea, I felt I was abandoning a very basic principle of his upbringing.

I would go to bed fairly early firstly so that I got lots of sleep and secondly I wouldn't be laying awake listening, waiting for him to get home. He was a real going out kind of guy, very rarely staying home in the evening and although it was difficult to keep up this regime at first I felt I had to. If only to show us both that I was trying not to be checking up on him and that was because I trusted him.

He never got into trouble with the cops, or any real trouble of any other kind. He was a mischievous, possibly over confident git but thankfully he never brought the law to the door. Apart from my good self that is.

A DECADE ON

I stood bawling my eyes out at Bristol Parkway Station as Gavin walked across the bridge to the platform for his train to Plymouth. He was wearing a smart dark suit and carrying what seemed an enormous bag. He'd been accepted for the Royal Navy and was now making his way in life too. My tears were of overwhelming pride. He gave me a card to read once he'd left me at the station. He thanked me for everything and vowed to make me proud. He already had.

This young guy who'd just crossed the bridge has had one hell of a journey and so far dealt with it showing strength and maturity beyond his years. Now the rest of that journey is fully under his control as he posed for photos with friends, laughing and joking, this was his moment. I reveled in it too, much as I had in Lewis's moment at his wedding, in the background but there all the same. As I always will be.

As I strode across the blurred car park from the station towards what I hoped was my car I, like him, was striding into a new life or more accurately a new phase of my life.

I stood, reluctant to get in until his train had pulled out. I didn't have to wait for long as the intense growl of the engine increased and the shiny red and silver train emerged into the warm sun, pulling away into the future and carrying a cargo so precious. He would, no doubt, have tough times in the future, even more so during his training and I would always be at the end of the phone. He would nevertheless have to find solutions for himself too.

I waved at the train until it was out of sight. I couldn't help drawing comparisons with my feelings as Lewis and Liz walked down the aisle into their future.

Through the tears and fog of emotions I thought of my Dad and my Grandad. I desperately hoped they would have approved of the course I had chosen, and the decisions I had made in my life so far. I had in turn watched the boys move into new phases of their lives as independent adults. Phases that a decade ago I doubted I would witness without a fight, yet here I was having witnessed, and indeed been a part of both.

The day I left the family home a decade earlier and laid with the boys telling them I was leaving, I thought I was at my lowest point. However, my journey like that of many others went on to take me to darker, much more desperate places.

Now, following all the trauma I am completely at the other end of the scale, self-actualisation, and it certainly felt good, very good.

I was to retire from the police service just six weeks later and eager to take up the challenge of being self-employed. How many challenges do I need?

There was however one challenge awaiting at home before my new life could begin. His typically teenage, filthy, untidy pig-sty of a bedroom was now completely at my mercy, better stop off and get some more bin liners on the way home!

~

Wednesday 7 May, was always going to be a very special day. Not only because I was to fly to Scotland to take part in that year's 'The Great Outdoors Challenge.' This event being exactly a decade since the ill-fated attempt in 1998 and the start of the emotional journey that is this book. It was going to be the day I would hand in my police warrant card for good.

Taking part in the event required a great deal of planning and preparation and the day duly arrived when I was to get a lift to the station to begin my travels to the airport. It was pleasantly warm as I lay in the garden having lunch and a wee dram, satisfied that I was packed and ready. My rucksack was standing in the kitchen, looking ominously heavy.

Lunch over and as I opened the garage door to put away the sun lounger, I stood a while and admired the huge, shiny black and brand new Yamaha TDM 900 motorcycle. My recent purchase, a retirement gift from me to me with love!

Along with the golf clubs, it was evidence of my survival and more importantly that the boys were well, so I had time to enjoy my past times as well as the boys and their blossoming lives.

On the train and coach to the airport I cut a very contented figure. I had a great deal to be grateful for but without, I hope, sounding arrogant, I think I had earned the right to feel like this. I knew many guys for whom the single life would be sufficient. I also knew that for me it wouldn't be. I was never a 'Jack the lad' type and wondered if emotional contentment in the form of a long lasting relationship would again be mine in the future. Who knows, but never say never. The coach arrived at the airport. I was catapulted back into a very real present as I slung my rucksack on and walked to the police station.

As I was to be out of England and Wales on my actual retirement day I had to hand in my warrant card on my final day in England.

I sat at the airport police station and chatted over coffee with the Sergeant and a couple of the officers whom I had known for years. Soon my cup was empty and with the minimum of fuss I stood up and handed the two cards to the Sergeant. After a firm handshake and accepting the thanks for my efforts over the years, I picked up my rucksack and headed for the terminal.

The short walk, was a bizarre experience, I recall listening to my heartbeat and to every footstep. For the first time in over twenty five years I hadn't got a warrant card and it seemed so very strange. The sun was warm and with every step I was feeling better and better.

In a matter of six days and after a mere flick of a switch, I would be financially secure. There will be no more courts, no more attacks and no more 'Police Constable Reed.'

I'd booked my flight to Aberdeen on a small business commuter aircraft and enjoyed a couple of glasses of champagne in flight. As I made my way to exit the plane once landed the stewardess asked to my surprise, "Is it Mr Reed?"

"Yes" was my reply, "Oh shit what now." was my first thought.

She continued, "I didn't want to embarrass you but I believe you have just retired from the police service."

"Yes, how did you know?"

Her look clearly stated she wasn't about to reveal her source.

"On behalf of Eastern Airways, and others, thank you for your efforts and please accept this bottle of champagne."

I was stunned and yet delighted. I thanked her and made my way into the warm evening carrying an ice cold bottle of bubbly and an enormous smile across my face.

Throughout that evening her words kept ringing in my ears, "Thank you for your efforts."

To all those toward whom my efforts were directed; you are very welcome and to all those whose efforts were towards me; thank you for yours.

My thoughts turned to Lewis and Gavin, immensely proud of them both, two fine young men. The same core, with different outer qualities, now go forward, strong, honest, dignified and with pride in who you are. I believe I did them proud.

The Road to Success...

The road to Success isn't Straight,

There are Curves called Failure,

A Loop called Confusion,

Speed bumps called Friends,

Red lights called Adversaries,

Caution lights called Family.

You will have flat Tyres called Jobs

BUT,

If you have a Spare called Determination,

An Engine called Perseverance,

Insurance called Faith and,

A Driver called Love,

You will make it to a place called

SUCCESS.

Lightning Source UK Ltd.
Milton Keynes UK
UKOW06f2310170815

257065UK00009B/141/P